Learning to Hope

Learning to Hope

*The Church and the
Desire for Wisdom*

Kenneth Wilson

EPWORTH

British Library Cataloguing in Publication data

A catalogue record for this book is available
from the British Library

0 7162 0627 7/978 0 7162 0627 9

First published in 2006
by Epworth Press
4 John Wesley Road
Werrington
Peterborough PE4 6ZP

Printed and bound in Great Britain by
William Clowes Ltd, Beccles, Suffolk

Contents

Preface

Has the person yet been born who has not been drawn to ask whether life has meaning? Personally, I doubt it. For myself, I can hardly remember a time when I was not puzzled and curious about life's meaning. What is more, life becomes more intriguing and puzzling, it seems to me, as one gets older. Indeed, it is one of the best things about life; it gets better as you get older.

The Church has, to its detriment, sought from time to time to domesticate this natural curiosity by appearing to define the meaning of life. It has written it down in official manuals, catechisms and books of instruction. The Church began the practice in its early history because it was necessary to instruct newcomers to the faith. It was vital to secure their understanding of and commitment to the new religion of Jesus Christ, the Lord. There was a particular reason for doing this. To confess the faith of Christ could be a very dangerous thing: it still is in some places. In principle, of course, it always is, for 'true teaching disturbs complacency'.[1]

At first no doubt the instruction was oral and only later written. It would have been brief and largely based upon the words of Jesus and the Apostles' Creed. Latterly, catechetical material has varied in size. *The Catholic Catechism* was a substantial undertaking; it was commissioned by Pope John Paul II in 1986, following a decision of the Extraordinary Synod of Bishops in the previous year which asked for a full expression of the faith of the Church in the light of the teaching of Vatican II. The publication date in French was 1992, with an English translation two years later.[2] In 2006 there was published the *Compendium of the Catechism of the Catholic Church*, briefer than the Catechism, but still substantial at 200 pages. The Anglican catechism is very much briefer and with a different purpose was an innovation in the Prayer Book of 1549; it was revised in 1961 and is now omitted in *Common Worship*, while the *Adult Catechism* of the Methodist Church is more modest still.[3]

This book, while concerned with the teaching of the Church, focuses upon the Church as the Learning Community. The Church, the people of God, is alive in so far as it is talking through, and living out, its faith in the world. There is no final end in sight to talking and living: the Living Church, called into being by the Word of God, will always be 'learning to hope' and hoping to learn.

Hope is trivialized when we abandon reason and ground it in unwarranted dysfunctional optimism. True hope arises from an interest in the gamut of human experience and knowledge of the world, its nature and possibilities; it leads to fruitful policy in personal and public life. If our hope is to be sustained in the face of difficulty and disappointment, we shall need, above all, honest and creative relationships that are best nourished in open, courteous conversation with our peers and with God. Hence my concern here with learning to hope.

Introduction: Learning

Every parent knows how natural it is for a child to learn – almost anything and everything, good and bad; this makes it all the more important that there is some direction, some focus to the learning. Yes, children will acquire what we would call 'information', but they also set about from the earliest age 'testing the limits' to see 'what will happen if . . .' Absorption of 'facts', learning from 'experience', and finding out by 'experiment', are all features of every child's life.

Parents play a key role in shaping, encouraging and even directing this natural capacity into the most useful and rewarding paths: they can succeed or fail in this enterprise but failure is a serious matter. Teachers know only too well just how much of a problem children can be to them if their parents have given them no sense of achievement and provided little if any stimulus to learn. The family is a key 'learning community' in the fullest sense of the term, because so much of what a child learns at an early stage is absorbed from the social and linguistic environment in which the child is beginning to find a path to follow: the way in which a family 'learns together' will be of lasting significance.

The problem created by ill-disciplined learning is complex and multi-dimensional, for learning itself is a complex and disparate set of processes. Learning, for example, is not simply a matter of acquiring factual knowledge, important though that is. To mention only a few of the other aspects of learning, they embrace critical awareness, technical skill, the stimulus of the imagination, the development of moral sensitivity, the formation of character in the widest perspective and the lively opportunities provided by the worlds of the aesthetic: music, painting, sculpture and landscaping. These are not, of course, discrete areas. No scientist will be creative if he lacks imagination, a sense of beauty and a commitment to integrity as an enquirer. No artist will be able to find expression for her vision without knowledge of materials, techniques, honesty of vision and, in addition, a basic appreciation of the action of light on a picture, or a piece of sculpture. There are not only matters of fact involved here, since the scientist and the artist both alike require the exercise of an educated judgement that flows from experience. In the end the development of educated judgement depends upon motivation, the capacity to concentrate, and the gaining of discernment that comes from a willingness to give oneself to the business of learning.

I say '*give oneself* to the business of learning' advisedly, for learning is a whole-person activity. One does not learn with a bit of oneself, or if one does, one will only understand – or perhaps better 'see' – one or two aspects of what one is trying to learn. It is now fashionable, for example, once again to require children to learn their multiplication tables. 'Two twos are four, three twos are six, and four twos are eight, so what are five twos?' If the child has been paying attention to what he or she sees or has been told, then the sequence will have been identified and he or she will find it possible to work out that 'five twos are ten'. Indeed there will be a real personal pleasure associated with having seen what it is all about, from which will stem new motivation and further desire to learn. This personal pleasure in learning will be reinforced by the appreciation of the teacher but will not be capable of being reduced to it; the pleasure of learning is real, long-lasting and personally creative. On the other hand, if all the child has been focusing on is trying to remember the sequence of sounds or the appearance of the words, then he or she will not have understood the process, be unable to work out the answer, and therefore *a fortiori*, derive no pleasure from the process.

In this context it is important to realize that remembering is not just the printing of a piece of information in the brain, it is an activity. It is a matter of having the information available for us so that we can link it with other information and for that to be the case it is essential that one has digested it; indeed it has, as we say, to have become part of us. We have to know that we know: this way lies confidence.

I say 'give oneself to *the business* of learning' because in a profound sense successful learning is like a successful business. A successful business will not simply focus on its immediate product (though it had better not lose sight of its importance); it will be looking at the marketplace to see what new products should be researched, developed and manufactured, it will examine its production systems and patterns of investment, it will be looking at the similar products of competitors, and even be seeking mergers and acquisitions in order to grow its share of the market – for all of which capital is necessary, together with investment in research, staff development and retooling, etc. Learning also requires clear purpose, investment of time and resources, hard work, and consistent application. But when it is successful it produces the profit of enlarged horizons, deeper understanding, stimulated curiosity and clearer focus on what matters, all of which are necessary conditions for the growth of capital – by which in this case I mean personal capital.

The learner, as he or she learns more, becomes open to the wider relationships and therefore potential applications of his or her particular knowledge. For example, the development of the fluitship in the Netherlands in the sixteenth century was not the incidental consequence of experiments by intelligent ship designers. The fluitship was a broad-bellied cargo vessel that carried a new rig, and remained comparatively stable in troubled waters – it carried larger cargoes, and was therefore more profitable than the smaller if sometimes faster boats operated by British owners. Moreover the Dutch understood the economics of population growth in Europe before anyone else and realized that the Polish production of cheap grain was vital to the feeding of Europe. (It's interesting that in the contemporary EU British farmers are beginning to experience again the production potential of European enlargement with the accession, very particularly, of Poland.) Knowledge of physics, meteorology, astronomy, geography, economics and agriculture, among other things, all add to the explanation of the fluitship's success and the massive contribution it added to the political and economic prosperity of the Dutch during the sixteenth and early seventeenth centuries through its control of the trade in grain and timber in the Baltic. The zenith of the Dutch success was 1618. The imaginative extension of the range over which any knowledge can be useful makes the learner more self-aware, more aware of others, and more capable of working with others for the well-being of all.

Personal capital may seem a curious concept, but I think it is important to grasp its significance. We talk regularly now of 'social capital' and are inclined to be gloomy about its reduction. It is all very well to talk of a company's financial capital, but increasingly we talk of the capital value, often hidden in the private conversations, and even the grumbles, and locked up in its employees.[1] Their commitment, imagination and sheer hard work are very important, but there is also the vast ocean of ideas and suggestions flowing from their experience of the way the company operates, which, were the company to find ways of releasing them, might transform not only the efficiency of the existing operation, but bring to light new products, new production methods and more efficient management structures. Any company worth its salt knows how easily it can dissipate its social capital and takes steps to minimize it. Too many, however, focus on other dimensions of the business. They may even be unaware of the importance of social capital, fail to invest in it and offer no opportunities for its expression; it may not, for example, take appropriate steps to avoid rapid turnover of staff and focus rather on share price at the expense of everything else.

Social capital in the much wider reference of community is perhaps even more crucial to the flourishing life of society and even more easily ignored and lost. I was a probationer minister at Hinde Street Methodist Church in London's West End from 1964 to 1966 and observed during that time the dissipation of local social coherence when whole localities were destroyed. I remember the case of Luxborough Buildings. It was certainly not the most handsome of properties, nor was the ambience of the accommodation attractive or particularly comfortable, but there was the welcome coherence of a caring community and the ever-present sense of mutual support. This was dissipated when the residents were rehoused in high-rise developments or scattered to small communities for the elderly in the suburbs. One should not romanticize the colours of such 'old' communities, for no doubt investment was necessary after the austerity of the Second World War and the new accommodation was certainly superior, but neither should one ignore the impact of the changes to a community when apparent indifference to personal needs leads to a loss of identity. Friends were lost, access to shops was put out of reach and it became very difficult in many cases for families to make the journey to visit relatives and friends. Mary Douglas, the distinguished social anthropologist, argued at the time that social investment, including free telephones and subsidized public transport, should be part of extended welfare in order to maintain conversation and the stimulus to life which comes from the regular revitalization of memory.

When social capital is reducing one is likely also to lose the capacity to build personal capital because one is dependent upon the other. The loss of community may lead to the emergence of private capital because one can come to believe that one's well-being depends upon oneself, but that has nothing to do with the development of personal capital or therefore the well-being of a community as a learning society. Private capital is what I own and believe I can control for my own benefit; personal capital depends for its flourishing upon membership of community and above all the ability of the individual to benefit from, contribute to and share in its flourishing. Communities, like persons, enjoy an ability to grow in wisdom and self-awareness: a community can build community value.

The fact that one can build personal capital – and thus the ability through finding oneself to contribute to the social capital – underlines the fact that learning is a voluntary activity; it is something that we do for ourselves, like blinking, that no one else can do for us. I recall a former colleague who once wrote on a pupil's Latin report, 'You can take a horse to water but you cannot make it drink'. He was right. If the pupil is not interested to learn something, and is utterly unwilling to apply himself, then that is that. No threat of punishment can sufficiently motivate any of us so that we apply ourselves to learning something that we perceive, rightly or wrongly, to be valueless. That a student cannot be commanded to learn, every teacher and parent knows: neither, of course, can anyone *at any age* reasonably order someone to learn something and expect it to happen. All this points to the fact that learning is personal and takes place in community; it implies a growth in self-awareness and therefore also in the awareness of others.

Learning is, as I said above, a whole-person activity. Self-awareness is a product of the many-faceted matter of learning. We do not just learn about the world around us. Because we constitute a dimension of the world about which we are learning we are also, as we learn, learning about ourselves. Moreover, we are not simply a product of what we learn. We put things together which in the world are separate, we determine what is more or less important, we build them into imaginative interpretative structures – mathematical, historical, sociological, anthropological, scientific – such that it is necessary for us to exercise judgement. We contribute to our understanding of what it is to be a self through the ways in which we embrace, co-ordinate and build our knowledge into coherent patterns and judge between them. We are in a profound sense modellers; that is, modellers of ourselves as well as of the experience of the 'outside' world which we are interpreting.

This capacity to model raises questions for us about ourselves, and what it is to be human. Who are we that we can even begin to *understand* the world of which we are inextricably a part? What does it say about what it is to be human, and to be me? Isn't it remarkable that the brain of a human person can entertain a view of the whole of the known world from, say, t-40 of a pico second from its origin until now, and anticipate the potential circumstances and the timescale for the total life of the universe? To lose the excitement of learning and the desire to invest time and energy – and indeed *oneself* in trying to learn, trying to make sense of one's experience – is simply to choose to ignore vital dimensions of what it is to be human and in fact to choose to die.

This aspect of learning is not just true of persons as individuals; it is also true of communities. Communities that have ceased to learn, that for example do not remind themselves of their history – of their stories, as we are now inclined to say – will, like individuals, lose a sense of their own identity. The rapid social, political, economic, cultural and religious changes that we are experiencing at the present moment throughout the world, but especially in Europe, illustrate the point that I am making. Nicholas Boyle is Schröder Professor of German at Cambridge University, and writes from a Roman Catholic perspective. He called the splendid book in which he faced up to the twin challenges of growing plurality and greater unification, *Who Are We Now?*[2] In a series of illuminating essays he focused particularly on the very relevant matters of Germany and Britain. Britain has, as Foster Dulles once remarked, lost an empire and failed to find a role; Germany has yet to come to terms with the consequences of the fall of the Russian Empire and German reunification.[3] When the traditions and securities and inherited values (often unquestioned) that we have been used to are no longer the common property they once were, it is a question that faces each of us. Who are we now? Who am I? Where have we come from and where are we going? We are thrown back on to our own resources.

We may, of course, turn to build a 'new' Europe, or 'New Labour'; we may call ourselves a multicultural, multifaith or multiracial society; we may try to think ourselves into a global economy with a 'human' face rather than a national identity; we may want to think ourselves into a postmodern environment where we recognize that there is no valid overarching narrative; but it is clear from the way in which we react that none of these statements is accepted as the whole truth, for each raises uncomfortable questions. We do not yet know how to learn in the new situation because we do not yet understand or intuit clearly what we want to learn, let alone what we need to learn, if we are to become what we are and realize our own identity. There is even more to it than this. The publishers quote the illuminating words of Vaclav Havel in their blurb to Nicholas Boyle's book, 'It cannot suffice to invent new machines, new regulations, new institutions. It is necessary to understand differently and more perfectly the true purpose of our existence on this Earth and of our deeds.'

On this matter the Christian Church has something to say that is of profound importance. But Christians have to be free to say it, and in order to be free to say it we Christians shall have to discover the freedom to learn. Freedom, as Hegel remarked, is not something with which we are born, but something we make. I suppose most people regard themselves as free to learn, and in principle rightly so. At the same time we have to admit that we do not always take the opportunities to learn that are presented and therefore grow in conventional acceptance rather than entering the free world where, as Christ promised, we are free to question and therefore free to learn.[4] The education system to which we are gradually becoming attuned is defined by a national curriculum, the required outcomes of which are inattentive to the qualities that underpin personal flourishing, because they focus upon providing a majority with individual, but private, economic prosperity. Schools and teachers are inspected, school performances ordered on published lists, and teachers focused upon recording and testing in such a way as to limit the attention that can be paid to personal development and, as I would say, character formation.

Inattention to the values of liberal education finds wide echo in political life. Anxiety over the undoubtedly real international terrorist threat, which must never be underestimated, has led and is still leading to legislation that increasingly threatens free speech. For example, in the most crucial area of religious belief the desire to legislate against the incitement of religious hatred is a case in point. Of course, incitement to hatred on grounds of religious belief is deplorable, it surely is on any grounds; however, that it should be the case that whether an offence is committed will depend upon the beliefs, feelings and attitudes of the 'offended' person is simply bad law. I am not particularly comforted by the assertion that whether any case is actually brought to trial will depend in the last resort upon the decision of the Attorney General, since his judgement will depend upon his personal philosophy and the general attitude of the government of the day. The wisdom of British society has emerged over a very long period through the serious debate in public of the values, beliefs and actions of its members. Not every belief is reasonable – most certainly not every religious belief is reasonable: it must be possible in public to assert this for all our sakes, and for the merits of the case to be debated.

Further, we might consider the Legislation and Regulatory Reform Bill, which reserves to ministers the right to change whole swathes of the law that hitherto have been the prerogative of Parliament. One of the reasons behind the supposed need for this 'reform' is the constant increase in the amount of legislation (some of it, of course, European), with all the associated poor drafting, which is itself a witness to the way in which government wrongly believes that society will be improved by the imposition of more bureaucratic accountability. We must be careful that we do not accede to popularist politics and allow the values on which the survival of *human* society depends, to atrophy. The danger will come from doing nothing. As a recent book has suggested, it may well be that the real threat to the values of the West are self-inflicted, and come from within.[5]

The churches have from time to time indulged in the same sort of activity. What is essential to Christian faith is the affirmation that the world is the creation of God, who accepts responsibility for its well-being and has committed himself to its success, so that those who work at what that means for the world's and human well-being see themselves as working with God for the fulfilment of his purpose in creating. What that means for social, political and economic organization we can only hope to learn by reflecting and building upon experience. We say that God created the world, that Jesus is the Incarnate Son of God, and that he rose from the dead and ascended into heaven where he sits on the right hand of the Father. Well, what, *on earth*, does that mean? It requires very hard work even to begin to get it sorted out. If we can. It is vital that we do keep working at it, as a community of faith as well as through the necessary work of individual scholars; we must keep the conversation alive and healthy if we are to grow into the freedom that participation in the faith offers. The importance of personal freedom for personal growth in faith and understanding is impossible to overestimate.

Yet, to question the physical resurrection of Christ, or his divinity, would be regarded by many as tantamount to questioning one's Christian faith. When it comes to trying to understand what it means to assert that 'God created the world', to some minds it is unchristian to accept evolution as the most illuminating way to interpret our understanding of the processes that underpin the scientific facts as we currently see them. I say 'currently see them' not because creationism might offer a reasonable fall-back position for believers which can be accepted alongside evolution, but because evolution is a scientific theory subject to correction and revision in the light of experience, whereas creationism is simply a doctrinaire statement unrelated to any useful information and irrelevant, therefore, to the way Christians might reasonably choose to live their lives.

The sensitive matter of homosexuality is driving the worldwide community of the Anglican Church towards schism, yet the matter must surely be debated with attention to current psychological understandings and the nature of human sexuality; answers cannot be deduced from simple readings from scripture. Pope John Paul II determined not only that women could never be ordained as priests, but that discussion of the question whether and for what reasons women should not be ordained would be proscribed *per se*. On all these, and all other matters, the Christian is endowed with the freedom to learn, but it is a freedom the individual must take, if he or she is to become free.

Not everything is open to us, not as a result of authoritarian proscription but because of the actual nature of human enquiry. As a matter of fact, it is this 'hiddenness' of some knowledge that illuminates the process of learning and the nature of knowledge, and perhaps indeed what the Christian might mean by revelation. What we learn reveals that there is a great deal that we take on trust, or at least have to assume for the purpose of coming to terms with what we are learning. Michael Polanyi called this the 'tacit dimension'.[6] The point is that we build much on hunches, have to entertain guesses, have to take responsibility for the sense we make of our experience, and attribute a great deal to the confidence built on long experience. So, as Polanyi discussed in his Gifford Lectures, the consultant when diagnosing the condition of the patient from the presenting symptoms relies to a considerable extent upon his or her experience, since the symptoms may suggest several possibilities. Of course, the consultant should never therefore draw the transcendental deduction and believe without caution that his or her present judgement is the one and only correct diagnosis. Actually, in the light of the patient's response to initial treatment or the later presentation of other symptoms, the consultant may want to revise the opinion.[7] The Christian doctrine of revelation is to be understood analogically with this perspective. It is not that God has revealed what we must believe, but that by his presence he makes it plain that whatever we think we know about the world, ourselves and God, there is always more to be known and, what is more, that can be learned. A great new performance of a Bach prelude and fugue is not imposed upon the material, but gives rise to new appreciation of the depths with which the music is engaged. Likewise, a new response to our human experience is not simply the organization of existing information and the imposition on it of a new interpretation, if it is significant it will 'add value' to the depth of our appreciation and enjoyment of the world we share.

Simone Weil talks of 'paying attention', learning how to give oneself to the matter in hand without regard for oneself, one's reputation or any surrounding potential distractions. But even she is aware that 'learning to pay attention' assumes a great deal of prior learning, which is necessary if one is to put into context what it is that one is paying attention to. Actually, the learning to pay attention, to give oneself to something or someone, is precisely what I am referring to when I suggest that learning is a whole-person activity. For when one is really 'paying attention' one is liberated, becoming free to learn, and beginning to enjoy (again) the welcome and pleasurable business of 'active learning'. All of this is further evidence of the dimension of the community in learning and the importance of community wisdom, for either the community will encourage the individual freedom to learn on which its own freedom depends, or it will constrain the individual and thus frustrate personal enquiry.

To learn is hard work. In simple terms we all recognize this. However, it is not only a product of the complexity of the subject matter, or the difficulty of identifying what it is to which we should be paying attention if we are to make sense of a topic, it also involves moral, characterological perspectives on our human personal behaviour. Thus, the willingness to attend again to matters we have found difficult on several attempts in the past, where we recognize that we have often made errors in approaching them, and despite repeated effort we cannot put our finger on where, requires courage. When, as will be most likely the case, we are working with colleagues, we shall require loyalty. Perhaps above all, we shall require two qualities that combine the Greek and Christian traditions. First, there is the quality of life that Aristotle believed was characteristic of human being, *curiosity* – which only in very specific circumstances can be said to have killed the cat! Second, there is the spiritual dimension of love, which the Christian faith adds while accepting a primary role for curiosity. We have to love the world in all its dimensions if we are serious about trying to understand; fear of the world or what we might learn is out of the question. We have also to love those persons with whom we are trying to enquire about the nature of human experience. The persons with whom we are involved cannot be limited, for they include in principle everyone; for from the Christian point of view each person has a unique value and must therefore be assumed to have made a unique contribution to the human conversation, whether recorded or not. And indeed one should say, whether good or bad, for we must hope that as human beings capable of learning from experience we can apply the lessons so learned. And we have to love God, as revealed in Christ and celebrated in the worship of the people of God, whose life and love lies behind and informs all that is.

In this pursuit we share with the best of Hellenism, that is, the classical Greek world of Socrates, Plato and Aristotle, and of Aeschylus, Sophocles and Euripides, its sense of the virtues of human life. These are the intellectual virtues of wisdom, intelligence and practical wisdom; the moral virtues of courage, temperance and justice, truthfulness, liberality, good temper, amiability, right ambition; and the social virtue of urbane wit, the quality which 'makes society work' which is neither inanity nor rudeness, but the participate liberality engendered by the generosity of a fruitful education. These virtues will wither and die if not regularly nourished. It was the understanding of both Plato and Aristotle, and witnessed to in the writings of Thucidides, the first great historian, that the role of the state was to provide the environment whereby the citizen could discover the good life, the virtue (the *arête*, or perfection) of what it was to be human.

The Christian knows that the love, which is part of his or her experience, is characteristic of the divine presence in the world and makes the good life possible. But uniquely the Christian understands too that there is a good deal of unlearning that has to go on if he or she is to realize the potential that is implicit in this understanding. For it is apparent that each person is inclined to rely on his or her own strength and understanding, to ignore his or her dependence on others even for that basic tool of language, let alone human dependence upon the rest of the natural world and most particularly on God. It is as if we could understand the world without language, for which, of course, we require the society of others, but still learn all that we need to know in order to flourish by talking to ourselves. We obviously cannot; even viruses, we are now discovering, have complex and very subtle means of communication that mean they hunt in packs and not as individual organisms! Learning to unlearn is one of the hardest skills to acquire, but its acquisition is essential for *human* survival.

It is clear from everything we have said that learning is essential to human flourishing; that we depend upon one another; that the focus of what we are wanting to learn, and trying to learn, is an indication of our character because learning is a whole-person activity that we can participate in if we want to. It must also be clear that learning is a risky business; there is no comfort zone. For myself, that seems to be good reason to thank God, for far from protecting us against the potential evil that might flow from our acquisition of new knowledge, he freely opened up his/our world to our enquiry, and committed himself to accompanying us in the exercise of judgement whereby we can find life, not just in the here and now, but for all eternity. What *that* means is worth some thought, too! Certainly, however, it means that since we can hope to learn, we have good grounds for believing that we are justified in claiming that we are learning to hope.

There is no dimension of human experience that is excluded from our Christian conversation with God as we try to make his world a place of faith. For this to be the case, however, the Christian community has to engage with the whole gamut of human experience. Like Terence, the Latin poet, we have to learn what it means to say, and act as if we believed, that 'nothing that is human is alien to us'. So let's begin the conversation with our Christian appreciation of the world as God's creation.

Let's Talk About Creating

Have you ever wondered about the inspiration of the artist – where it comes from, how the artist goes about producing a painting or sculpture, what he or she 'sees' and how it is presented? One thing seems clear; a work of art is the result of deliberate choice, not accidental behaviour. Creating, like learning, is not the activity of an automaton: it is essentially a voluntary activity; it is something a person must want to do. Our ordinary human experience confirms this.

The product of every creative enterprise, whether it be music, art, scientific theory, or a historical interpretation, has an author – that is, a *personal* origin. An *objet trouvé* can be very intriguing but it is not a work of art. There again, if a puppy happens to sit on a page of writing that still has wet ink, even if the result is curiously attractive, we would not want to use the term 'create' to cover the puppy's behaviour. In no way could the dog be said to have acted intentionally, or to have given personal expression to its vision of its world. The puppy could not, for instance, be said to have wanted to share anything or give pleasure to other puppies. Neither could it be said, in its perplexity about the meaning of its life, to have been struggling to give it form in order to contribute to the search for meaning and purpose in puppydom. In other words, the puppy is not a creator; a puppy is not a person.

Painters are, on the other hand, self-consciously reflective about their experience of the world. They make decisions about the subject of the picture; they choose the medium, the materials, the style, the texture and the colours to be employed. Actually, whether they are self-taught or whether they have been to school and studied the traditions of artistic enquiry, they will have reflected on the way they wish to depict what they 'see' and how best to express their feelings in the finished product. Moreover, what every great artist shows in a painting will, in one way or another, be, or certainly include, himself or herself. Crucially, it must be emphasized, this showing of the self in art is not independent of the perception of the world as the artist sees it, for it is the unique combination of objective perception and self-expression that makes a work of art the personal creation of an individual artist's vision.

There is another aspect to consider in respect of every creative endeavour. One might put the question this way: 'Where does one begin and how does one know when one has finished?' Actually, in a very important sense a work of art has no beginning and is never finished. Of course I can tell you the day and the hour at which I sat down to commence writing this book and I hope I shall be able to inform you on what day I stopped typing it on my computer, but that is not the point. A work of art may gestate in the mind and the heart for years and draw on a lifetime's experience of thinking, working, and feeling. It will, however, only begin to take form when, as the result of some stimulus, the artist is prompted to make the decision to start work, and only end when he or she recognizes the fact that he or she can do no more on his or her own. The significance of the phrase 'on his or her own' is one to which I shall want to return later.

In any creative activity, perhaps the hardest thing to do is to decide when to stop and when to hand it over to the world for which, in principle, the artist has always intended the work. How did Jane Austen know when to stop writing *Mansfield Park* or George Eliot, *Middlemarch*? Did Charlotte Bronte have in mind her famous words that open the final chapter of *Jane Eyre*: 'Reader, I married him', from the very inception of the novel, or did she struggle to find the right sentence after all else was practically complete? Did Marcel Proust think he knew how long *Remembrance of Things Past* would be when he first put pen to paper? Or for that matter, how did he know when he had finished what turned out to be eight volumes (in the French edition)?

Beginnings are very important. A painter will want to think very carefully about where on the canvas to make the first brush-mark, because it will influence the perspective, the composition, the range of colour and the ultimate capacity of the observer to engage with the painting. It is the same with a novelist or playwright: the beginning is crucial. Samuel Beckett's *Waiting for Godot* concerns two tramps who are doing just that, waiting for Godot. Beckett begins with Estragon sitting in the middle of the stage giving his whole attention to a superhuman effort to tie his shoelaces. Estragon fails, and he says to Vladimir, 'Nothing to be done'.[1] The ambiguity of those words opens up the drama, transforms it and at the same time sums up the whole matter of the play. The punctuation is important: there's no exclamation mark. Estragon offers no surprise; it's no expression of resentment, just a simple statement of fact: 'Nothing to be done'. And by the way, if you are familiar with the play, what exactly is its subject matter? Isn't the question raised by the tired opening sentence itself the dramatic point of the play? Isn't it this that makes the play perpetually puzzling for every participant member of the audience, reader, critic and co-creator? Is life anything more than this?

It is a tale
Told by an idiot, full of sound and fury,
Signifying nothing.[2]

Except that in this instance as Beckett sees it, there is not much sound and absolutely no fury.

It was T. S. Eliot who wrote revealingly, 'In my beginning is my end'; so it is, properly understood.[3] It is to tackle what this might mean that the artist on behalf of all humanity engages with the business of elaborating the question(s) raised in human experience, if not with the proffering, let alone the definitive stating of answers. After all, answers bring about the death-dealing finitude of certainty, whereas as life progresses we find ourselves to be part of an open system of enquiry in which, through participative articulation of our experience, we share the work of creation. Hence my remark above about the work of art only being complete when the artist decides to hand over the new creation to the world. There it will, if it is lively and revealing, stimulate interest in the question of beginnings, and enter into the conversation of the generations – which is how that most stimulating of philosophers, Michael Oakeshott, described education: 'Education in its most general significance may be recognized as a specific transaction which may go on between the generations of human beings in which newcomers to the scene are initiated into the world they are to inhabit.'[4]

If in my beginning is my end, what can we say about it? How can we talk about it? How can we become responsible for it? How can we get the hang of what's going on and take our part in the story? What can we do to enjoy it, share it and explore it with others? Where do we position ourselves in relation to our world if we are to be able to respond sensibly and build creative interpretations of it?

Christians, I believe, approach their experience of the world in a similar manner. 'In our beginning is our end'. First, we affirm with our whole being that the world in which we are set and of which we are a part is created. By so doing we are at least asserting that our experience of the world is analogous to that of an artist in relation to a work of art: like every artist, we feel a part of, and yet set apart so as to be capable of observing, our world. When Van Gogh, for example, looked at the woods and fields about Arles the excitement he felt at the colours, shapes and perspectives aroused in him not just the possibility of making a picture to be got down on canvas as an exact copy – that would have been impossible in any case. What he saw was a world of which he was a part that he wanted to make something of and share with the rest of humanity. He was about the business of creating. Have a look, for example, at two of the landscapes he produced at Arles in 1888, *View of Arles with Irises in the Foreground* or *Orchard in Bloom with Arles in the Background*.[5] Had any landscape before appeared like this to anyone? Never, it is safe to say. Yet once one is familiar with Van Gogh's vision of the world, given similar light and countryside, the viewer sees every landscape with fresh eyes. Colours are more daring and more subtle, the contrast of shape and form greater, the place of human being in the world raised in new ways, the relation between foreground and the distance more illuminating, and the detail more profound: we may even talk of experiencing a work of art as revelation. And it isn't just landscapes; take a look at the portraits of the Roulin family which Van Gogh painted the same year, 1888. These reveal an ordinary family – that is, ordinary families, real families, our families, in relationship despite their presentation in separate pictures.

And observation, contemplation of such works of art, arouses a sense of gratitude for the new light thrown on our shared world. It is not just that we see things differently because we see different things *in* the world, but that as the result of our relationship with the artist and a sympathetic involvement with his world through his pictures, we have more to take into our experience than we had before. We are enlarged by our intelligent attention to the work of art. What is more, our imaginations are consequently stimulated to make raids of our own on familiar landscapes and familiar people, notwithstanding our lack of the technical skill, the materials or the opportunity to effect them. We search for new likenesses, new encouragement, and new revelation within and behind what we are looking at, in full confidence that we shall always be pursuing, but never arrive at, the illusory image of 'what it is really like'. The whole experience may be said to 'draw us out of ourselves' and, as Simone Weil says, teach us how to give attention to something that is other than us, so that we are freed to feel as ourselves, think for ourselves and continue the task of trying to find ourselves in the real world. Through this infinitely delightful process we may be said to be involved in the world's liberation. We share, as it were, in the creation of the world and the creation of ourselves in an inseparable and essentially interactive process in which we engage not as lonely private individuals but as persons-in-community. Come to think of it, forget 'as it were', because it is rather that we actually do share in creation by this process. But more of this later.

You may well ask at this point, what has this to do with God, the redemptive Creator of all that is? Everything! Here is one way in which to approach the question which, I believe, offers a sensitive, open, theological framework for our interpretation of human experience. We experience the world as a given, but which as a given is delightfully puzzling. What is more, notwithstanding that it sometimes appears threatening, it provokes positive enquiry and experiment, provokes diverse emotional responses, and invites participative judgement and action. Christians believe that God is responsible for the world in all its given-ness. The fact that we know the world to be responsive to enquiry so that it delivers information and presents an active, healing responsiveness to human life, leads Christians to claim that the world is the result of a freely chosen act of God whom, therefore, they can only conceive of in personal terms.

God did not have to create the world; God chose to do so. As Christians say in theological language, the world exists by God's grace. In so saying, of course, we are not simply asserting that it came into existence through God's free will but that it continues to exist, and always will be held in being through God's grace. By this we mean that it is through God's continuous, creative, personal relationship that the world has life. This, on a daily basis, is how human beings understand God. After all, it makes no sense to the Christian to say that God would do something at a particular time and place as if God could be God as Christians understand him and be the origin of the world's beginning but not responsible for the way in which it is working out.

God in creating is asserting and confirming the indelible nature of his relationship with the world he is making; it is, therefore, what in philosophical terms one might call an ontological relationship. The 'inside' of this enlivening perspective on what it is for God to be God is expressed in the single coherence of doctrines – creation, redemption, incarnation, crucifixion, resurrection and ascension. 'In the beginning is the end' – the doctrines only unpack in the light of Christian experience what is implicit in the fact of God's creatively redemptive commitment to the success of what he has involved himself with, namely his creation. What begins in God, has its fulfilment in God.

I suggested earlier that the newness of the opportunity provided by any work of art remains fresh at every moment, but only if the artist has the courage to hand his or her creation over, to let it go to find its own way in the world. God's activity as Creator has much in common with the artist in this respect: God can only do so much on his own with what he has in mind, he has then to launch it and look for co-operation, partnership, and imaginative insight with the world to which in affectionate concern he has always intended to hand over his creation. It is of the essence of 'creating' that one learns to hand over what one is trying to make. Of course, by 'handing over' I do not mean 'give away', for God's relationship with his work is eternal.

By the doctrines referred to above – creation, redemption, incarnation, crucifixion, resurrection and ascension – we assert that God has committed himself to making a success of his world, and that this commitment is absolute, personal and unthreatenable. Nothing will make God give up on the world, or on any aspect of it, most particularly on any human being who is focused on working for the success of what God has begun. Theologians have found ways of talking about God that try to make plain God's relatedness to his world so as to arouse insight into God's *aseity*, that is, to God as God is in God's self. This is currently an unpopular way of talking, for what can we humans know of the divine, of God as God is in God's self? But think of it this way.

We say of God that he is omnipotent, and so he is. But what do we mean when we say that God is omnipotent? When we think of ourselves we recognize that we lack power; indeed, we are inclined to think that if we had more power to enforce our view of the world on others, the world would be a much better place. If only we had absolute power, the world would be perfect. We would be positively intolerant of cruelty, we would eliminate fear, we would disenfranchise those who do not understand the way things are; in fact the liberation of the world would be reduced to nothing more nor less than liberation for me. 'Not your will, Lord, but mine be done!'

Divine power has profoundly contrasting virtues. It may

be (who knows?) that God has absolute power in principle in the world and that this goes with what we implicitly tend to believe about what it is for God to be God. That may be, but in order to realize his purpose as redemptive Creator that is not how God thinks of God's self. For God the power that matters for God is power to make the world free, and that requires God to have power over God's self, and in this respect his power is absolute. Nothing has power over God except God, over how he is, who he is, and what he does. Nothing that occurs in the world of God's 'experience', nothing outside God in his loving nature, influences what God chooses to do in relation to his world. Hence when referring to God as Creator, we say that he made the world out of nothing; there is *no thing* which brought any influence on what God chose to do. The character of the creation depends exclusively and wholly upon the nature of God as God is in God's self.[6]

As the Perfect Artist, God is a Creator who wants a creation; he could have chosen not to create had he wanted to, but it would have been outside his nature to decide not to share his delightful quality of love with that which was other than God, with his world as we know it. The world is not, therefore, a set of automata operating in relation to one another but without any essential relationship to him the Creator; it is a set of potentialities, of mutually interactive sensitivities to which God has 'handed over' all that he had in mind. God has done all that is open to him to do of himself and all that it was necessary for him to do in order to achieve his purpose, which is what Genesis means when it says, 'And God saw everything that he had made, and indeed, it was very good.'[7]

Two aspects of his activity in the world demonstrate his omnipotence. First, he has the power over himself so as not to 'interfere' or to take over the process of creating, and second, the absoluteness of his personal commitment of *himself* to making a success of it. The conversation that begins in God, he opens up to and continues with his Creation in the Word through which he creates. It is given full expression in the redemptive Living Word of Jesus, whom we call the

Christ, the End that is implicit in the Beginning. God is eternally Creator, he is never a manipulator; he asks for co-creators, and is eternally available in order that all persons who desire to be co-creators can be so. The incarnation, crucifixion, resurrection and ascension are the formal, doctrinal expressions of the fact that nothing in heaven or earth can separate us from the love of God.

We also say of God that he is omniscient, by which we usually mean that God knows everything. But what do we mean by 'everything'? Omniscient – that is something we should certainly like to be! After all, if we knew which companies were going to be the most profitable, and where the new opportunities were in the equity market, we would be increasingly wealthy, and therefore free to gratify any whim at any time. If we knew the answers to every possible question of the many versions of *Trivial Pursuit*, we should always be the winner. Online poker seems a good bet at the moment – if only we knew the order of the cards! But, of course, the success of such all-embracing knowledge depends upon the ignorance of everyone else. And the sort of information we are talking about is very limited in its range and usefulness; it would give rise to little real advantage because it would offer little personal insight. Our success would not be educative because it would not bring wisdom and courage; it would be unlikely to stimulate our sense of being a 'person-in-community' because for it to be profitable for me it would have to be private to me; the usefulness of my knowledge would be dependent upon your ignorance.

When, on the contrary, we attribute omniscience to God, we open up a huge range of opportunity and personal interest. Whatever else God may be said to have knowledge of, the one essential matter of which he knows himself to have knowledge is himself. Indeed, had God not such complete knowledge of himself, we could never eliminate the thought that there could be some circumstance, some concatenation of events, which would cause him to react, as we might say, 'out of character'. It is because we believe that he does have full knowledge of himself, that we can have confidence that what God has set himself to do, what he is committed to do, will be achieved, because it depends upon God's nature, upon his grace. God will do what God says he will do in creating, because, as Christians believe, God's being, saying and acting are one and the same thing. It is interesting, isn't it, that God is said in Genesis to 'speak' the world into being; he creates through the Word. Moreover, the Hebrew word that means 'word', *dabhar*, means also 'event', and 'action'; what God is, God says and God does.

God has perfect self-knowledge, and therefore complete power over himself. Appreciation of this fact provides the insight on which Christian faith relies, for on it depends the truth of the claim that God is all-loving. For only if God is unthreatenable by external principalities and powers, can he be truly free to be himself, and can we be confident that his grace is ever-present to nourish and bless us. Moreover, thank God, his affectionate commitment does not depend upon our response, for God is who God is and does not depend upon our response to him for his sense of self-worth.

All this contrasts with our own experience of ourselves and of one another. We can react to circumstances and find that we have behaved in a manner that causes us to rethink our idea of our self. Perhaps I find myself puzzled by a subject set for an essay; I may be short of time because I have been working on something else, or perhaps enjoying myself playing snooker when I should have been working. And so *in extremis* I resort to the internet and come across a piece of work that looks rather good and instead of using it to equip myself to write an essay of my own, I submit it as if it were mine. I am accused of plagiarism and in my shame I try to explain myself by devious means, only to find myself exposed. Having never behaved like that previously, I might well be driven to reflect, 'I don't recognize myself, I did not think that I could behave like that and yet I have'. Such an experience is outside our understanding of what it is for God to be God: God can never behave out of character. Thus our God is able to give himself to that which is other than himself without diminishing himself and without threatening the essential integrity of that to which he gives himself. He is therefore, all the more importantly for us, able to understand our predicament and provide a personal framework in which we can recover a truer sense of ourselves, and through divine forgiveness, be reborn to new life in God's good creation.

Hence we can say with full confidence, universally and personally, God creates. God gives form to his creating; he gives himself to it (that is, makes himself available), so as to invite the curiosity, interest and participative activity of those, namely humankind, on whose willing and affectionate co-operation the continuing creativity of God's world depends. Is this to exaggerate the role that human persons have to play in the world? I do not think so. I am not claiming that the world is in human hands, for nothing that humankind can do will take away from God his ability to be himself. There is always, therefore, the possibility of new beginning, of new ways of looking at things, of new images of life, and new approaches to the human condition, because of the eternal life-giving presence of God. No, what God has handed over into human hands is the growing realization of the world of peace, justice, beauty and delight that is open to the whole creation through the unique contribution that humankind can bring.

It is of crucial importance to understand that implicit in what we are claiming about the totality of the world of our experience, is that God gives himself personally to all creation and not privately, as it were, to the Church. All humankind has the opportunity to contribute to the realization of God's purpose, not just Christians. The landscape of the world, including, of course, humankind, offers to all the possibility of knowing God, so as to stimulate the self-conscious personal apprehension of images that do not mirror the world exactly. I drew attention above to the fact that neither Van Gogh nor any other artist could ever produce an exact copy of what he saw; no more can any human being describe with completeness and accuracy every aspect of anything which he or she sees. What is open to us is much more interesting. We can share what we see, and build together a potentially revealing picture of the world, by working on the 'given' original through the images that we make in the light of our observations and our conversation about it. By so doing we engage in self-transforming processes, which extend our mutual vision of the world and the sense we have of ourselves as creative persons-in-relation with our world, with one another and with God. The process will never come to an end – at any rate in this life, and I personally believe not in the next either, because we cannot surely imagine that we can ever ransack God's being of his whole nature and, as it were, possess him.

The *given* world is alive with the freshness of God's love, which motivates our desire to learn. This key feature of our situation is expressed by Karl Rahner in the theological truth that there is no such thing as 'ungraced nature'; nor, I would add, therefore, is there any such thing as 'ungraced human nature'. The consequence of this is that from the very beginning of our lives we are curious about our world. We want to know what kinds of things there are, how they can be grouped together and classified, whether we can put them in some sort of hierarchy and if so what we can do with them. We are anxious to find out about our world, make sense of it, talk about it with others, hypothesize about its meaning, develop policies to guide our choices of behaviour as individuals and in society, and build programmes of action, which we review, change and adapt in the light of experience. And once we have begun, the effort is enchanting, almost literally – we cannot stop; enquiry is addictive. And best of all it involves others, for very early on if not exactly right from the beginning, we realize that we depend on others. It is not just that the world is given (as Christians believe, by God), but that any understanding we have of our experience depends upon what others are learning and saying, and must hang together with the stories told by others. The process of 'making sense' is a hugely fascinating and above all co-operative activity. We can be overcome by the attempt to put it all together.

It is not just that we want to understand it better, but that in the light of what we are learning we want to 'improve' it. Though this may be the wrong sort of language, let's stick with it for the moment. A small boy when given a new toy is likely to want to pull it apart and see how it fits together. But as soon as he has learned to do that with confidence, the thought will cross his mind that he could do better. Perhaps he could design it more efficiently with fewer parts; this could well be an accidental discovery, dependent upon the fact that it still works although there are three pieces left over! He may also discover a desire to make it more attractive by painting it a different colour. Or perhaps he is bored with the model car and reflects more generally on modes of transport; he could build a boat and try it out on the local pool. He may, of course, simply want to speculate and see if he can make something original and interesting with the pieces, though of supreme uselessness. It is fun, provides the opportunity to learn, to interact with the world, to discover what he can do, and what his personal resources of intelligence, imagination and perspicuity are.

But there is more. It is not only the discovery that there is a world 'out there' and the exploration of it so as to find out how it works and what the impact is on my self-understanding: there is the irresistible question of *why* it is like it is. The most complete answer to the 'how' question, even if (though impossible) it could be provided, would always be unsatisfying to our human nature. We want to know what is going on *really*. In principle this means that we want to know what we are involved in making – that is in 'creating' – as we set about the business of living and working in and with our world. The search for meaning, for what we can reasonably hope for in life, is embedded in every human culture; it is a common thread of every conversation between the generations. It is a dimension of this human living and thinking that bears fruit in the wide tradition of enquiry and practice we know as Christian. Of course, the human conversation does not begin with the Christian community. God's commitment to and conversation with the world begins in the beginning with God; so in the following chapter I try to place our Christian conversation into the larger context of God's People.

2

God's People:
Finding Our Way About

I have stressed the important point that we can never know precisely when or how anything begins. It is as true of the faith of the People of God as it is of the beliefs of any religious community or any other system of faith and practice. But who do Christians believe the People of God to be? The Canon Law of the Roman Catholic Church talks of 'Christ's faithful' as 'the People of God'.[1] No doubt in one sense this is true, as I shall explore below. However, I think we must first consider who 'the People of God' are in a much broader sense. This may seem strange given that we are talking primarily about the Church, but it should not. For in the profoundest sense in order to be true to the claims I have made on behalf of the Christian faith about the intimate relationship of the whole created order to the nature and being of God, we have to understand that as far as God is concerned, there are from the beginning only 'people'; that is, all persons are 'God's people'. God is concerned with all people, with their care, well-being and ultimate destiny. So when we stitch the Christian story into the fabric of the world of God's creating, there are no people (indeed, as we shall see later in Chapter 7 there is nothing at all) unrelated to the way in which Christians make sense of human experience. God is indeed the Redemptive Creator of all that is.

It is not surprising, therefore, that we should find archaeological evidence of religious practices and objects from the earliest emergence of human culture. Subsequently during the whole period of recorded time we find stories, theories, practices, myths, objects and associations that have emerged in the conversation developed by thoughtful human beings to explain their situation, to improve their lot, and to build hopes for the future. We humans have always 'wanted to know', 'tried to find out', and sought to put ourselves in a position where we could learn more and get better at the task of living a human life. But since in my view we are in principle precluded from getting right back to the beginning *per se*, I have no alternative but to choose where to take up the story of human enquiring. I shall place the emergence of our Christian thinking and believing in the context of the Jewish experience such as we find it in the Old Testament and follow its later development by Jewish scholars in the Talmud, Midrash and Hallachah.[2]

However, since the lively traditions of Judaism themselves did not spring fully formed out of nothing, even they need to be seen in context. If I was to attempt to do justice to the history of the vigour, curiosity and passion of the Jewish mind I would have to include reference to Canaanite religious practices, Babylonian creation stories, the Law Code of Hammurabi, Egyptian traditions, not to mention the later interactions of Judaism with Greek, Roman and Christian cultures. Even then I would hardly have begun. Moreover, ideas do not grow continuously or in a straight line; they ramify, they lie dormant from time to time only to re-emerge like old seeds in a new culture, they recombine like old inherited characteristics, they are interiorized in complex and different ways by different sections of society. Sociologists have helped us to understand this.

The merchant and the trader may share an interpretation of history, but the day-to-day lives of a nomadic tribe and of a settled community are likely to give rise to contrasting accounts. Men and women may have different life experiences and come up with related if different stories, but it would be a failure of understanding to assume that because women had no 'public' role they had no influence upon the stories the community told or the ideas associated with them as they developed. And so one could go on: the sailor, the tax-gatherer, the government official, the soldier, the lawyer, the priest, the young child, the potter, the hunter and the shepherd, all brought their experience to bear on the conversation in which Israelite society worked at the public understanding of its inheritance, its promises and its hopes. The conversation must go on today: the Christian community has the marvellous opportunity to extend the conversation of God with the world through engaging theological enquiry with the enormously extended range of experience, professional and personal, that make up our contemporary perspective.[3]

There is plenty of evidence of this in the various strands that make up the Old Testament. The Yahwistic and priestly traditions found in the Pentateuch provide the most obvious evidence of diversity, while David was a shepherd, Saul was anointed a king, and Ruth and Naomi were aliens abroad; each added a voice to the tradition. The prophets Jeremiah, Second Isaiah and the many contributors to the book of Psalms bear testimony to the contributions made through personal witness and individual advocacy. It's obvious really, though we are inclined to forget it; we know perfectly well, since on reflection honesty compels us to admit, that everyone we meet has something to contribute to our understanding, if we are willing to listen.

Clearly there is not space here to attempt such an all-embracing account even if it was possible, which it isn't. My purpose in alluding to it is to underline the open continuity of conversation that lies behind each societal 'organization' of thought, belief and practice and to make clear that in principle each person is a participant in the conversation between the generations and across the social groups. In commencing the account with the Jewish tradition, as I have chosen to do, I shall focus on six dimensions of human experience as filtered through the Jewish mind, largely drawing on the Old Testament; these are history, the natural world, morality and law, argument, suffering, and hope.

Judaism is a historical religion, not just in the obvious sense that like everything else that is human it has a place in history, but in the special sense that it believes history is a dimension in which God and humankind meet. Their evidence for this is based upon the story they tell of their own history. It was the Lord who called Abram, their progenitor, out of Ur, gave to him and his descendants for ever the land from the river of Egypt to the river Euphrates, blessed him with wife, servants and children and made a covenant with him (when he was 99!), changing his name to Abraham.

This calling does not seem to have brought peace, for right from the beginning there was confusion and conflict in the family. They seem to have wanted to test their vocation. Indeed, it seems that Abraham thought he was asked by God to sacrifice his son Isaac and actually set out to obey the commandment, only to be rescued by the intervention of God. Jacob and Esau, the sons of Isaac, did not see eye to eye. And all the time, according to Genesis, the Israelites had to make their way among the fearsome tribes of Canaan, to feed themselves as nomads in a land that was harsh, often dry and subject to drought, while doing their best to keep themselves to themselves and faithful to Yahweh.

Egypt, with the blessing of its beneficently flooding river Nile, could be a source of food in time of famine but as a result of one such embroilment the Israelites were captured, and only released by the crafty calculation and careful planning of Moses on God's advice – or so we learn in the book of Exodus. The Exodus became the ultimate ground of faith for the Jews, the ultimate proof that God was with them and that God's covenant with Abraham was absolute. The rest of their history, as the Old Testament has it, was a regular release of new energy and new faith, despite a natural tendency to disobedience and a commonsensical loss of faith when faced with crushing adversity. They were conquered by the Babylonians and taken into exile, yet even as exiles they knew God's love and returned to join those who had remained in Jerusalem. And the Temple that had been destroyed was rebuilt. It was not simply their religion, their prophets and at the last the faithful remnant that preached God's loving-kindness; their testimony was confirmed in the living experience of their history, in the personal lives of heroes such as Job, and embodied in the traditions that found expression in the Wisdom literature. God's gracious presence with and care for his people was for ever and ever.

There are several points to be drawn from this account. First, Israelite history interacts with a large number of tribes with whom in one way or another they had intimate relations. Second, the Israelites did not have an easy time of it; they had, in the face of enormous pressure, temptation and success, to work out their own salvation and to do so in all the many dimensions of their society. They had to make sense of things in the light of their faith; their faith did not make sense of things for them. They had to work out who God was, what faith in him actually meant, and how they were to be obedient to it. Third, there was their experience of the natural world, control over which was beyond them, and relationship with which was mysterious and sometimes threatening. Fourth, no matter where they placed themselves in relation to God, or how they viewed the world and their experience of it, they always seemed to come up with more questions that demanded attention. These might concern the success of the unbeliever, the failure of faith to bring rewards, the experience of defeat, and the ever-present reality of death and despair. And yet the Israelites worked at it so as to remain hopeful, not in their own strength, but in the light of their belief in the power, justice and presence of God whom, despite all evidence to the contrary, they believed stood behind the world and human history.

The Israelites soon recognized that they could not separate their experience of history from their understanding of the natural world. They may well have wanted to do so because in contrast to the tribes that surrounded them, their experience brought them first to put their trust in the 'God of history'. They were anxious, therefore, to distinguish themselves from the fertility religions and reductionist practices of worship on which the religions of neighbouring tribes centred. Nevertheless, they believed that God was the source of all life, and that therefore he gave the harvest on which their lives, like those of their neighbours, actually depended. But the way they thought through what this meant was different from their neighbours: the increase was natural, it did not depend upon the actual participation of Yahweh, nor therefore did Yahweh's participation depend upon the enactment of fertility rituals by the Israelites. Nevertheless, their historical experience of God's gracious presence implied some involvement of God with the natural world; indeed, the Israelites believed the Exodus itself involved a supernatural piling up of the waters of the Red Sea so that they could cross on dry land, and the engulfing of their pursuers in the subsequent flood.

They responded to this question by developing their own version of a creation story. God, the Creator, made his personal voice clear in the manner of his creating which was by his Spirit; he was involved with, capable of interacting with, but was in no way to be confused with, or assumed within, the world. The personal manner of his involvement with the Israelites in history was consistent with the manner of his personal relationship with the natural world. The two accounts we have in Genesis of the creation both affirm the uncompromising position of God: he it is who determines, from the very beginning, how things will be, and who is responsible. There could be no excuses for him. This insight provided the Israelites with the confidence that things should, could and would go well, and the stimulus to work at their (mis)understanding when things seemed to go wrong. And they did not mince their words; neither did they think they should. Since the world was God's creation, it was on their side – that is, in principle, on the side of humankind. So if and when things went wrong it was natural for them to vent their frustration by blaming God, and calling down hell and damnation on their enemies.

One way of approaching this is to say that for the Israelites, just as there was moral expectation implicit in their historical experience, given the covenant commitment of God to his people in creating them, so there was a moral expectation built into their understanding of God and their human experience of the natural world. God had promised, so there could be no question but that God would keep his promise and that they were justified in basing their lives on the belief that God would keep his covenanted promise. Signs such as the widow's cruse, stories such as Eli and God's calling of Samuel, and symbolic actions such as Jeremiah's buying Hanamel, his uncle's field in Anathoth, all enacted (that is, made real) the life-giving power of God and human beings in history and the natural world.[4] Above all, of course, this was apparent in the Exodus, as they reminded themselves every year at the Passover.

The announcement of order and pattern implicit in the manner of God's creating, combined with the Israelites' expectation aroused by God's covenant relation, led to the explicit definition of law by which their own lives could be ordered in relation to God's will for the world and for his people. The Decalogue interprets for their use their sense of Divine Order.[5] It has been suggested that the laws there instituted reflect the developed culture of a settled community and should therefore be associated with the seventh and eighth centuries BC rather than with the much earlier period of nomadic life in the time of Moses. However, the combination of ritual definition and moral legislation expressed in them has tended to bring scholarly opinion back to support the view that they originate in a Mosaic tradition. However that may be, the critical thing to understand is that conversation among the Israelites arising from what they understood to be the twin relation of God with the natural world and with history holds together the importance of ritual behaviour and moral sensitivity. Being right with God was a matter of avoiding idolatry, and also a matter of being right with your mother and father and, in the widest sense, with your neighbour.[6]

I choose argument as the fourth feature of Israelite life because the conventional view is that they were not concerned with reason and certainly not with anything that we would recognize as philosophy. The Israelites were concerned with faith in God and the ways of life that were consistent with belief in him, not with speculation about the nature of life, least of all about its origins. Clearly they were very interested in living life according to God's laws, to keeping his statutes and commandments; but that does not imply that they were uninterested in thinking through what that might mean for their understanding of God, of the world and of themselves in relation to fellow Israelites and to the rest of the human race in so far as they had contact with it or knowledge of it. Indeed, from what I have already said, it would be difficult to exclude them from the philosophical race.

Of course, the rise of professional philosophy has tended to remove that vital sense of philosophical enquiry as a way of life that was so powerful among the Greeks and has some echo in the writings of some Christian theologians such as Justin Martyr, Origen and Augustine.[7] Very particularly, Plato and Aristotle were concerned with the question of what sort of political socio-economic structure would be most conducive to the realization by human beings of 'the good life'. They thought of it in terms of the state.[8] Conversation on important matters would stimulate awareness of the world and self-awareness: the Academy was the environment where Plato talked and walked with his friends so as better and more clearly to understand those issues that were integral to the good life.

The Israelites thought of the good life in terms of their mutual relationships, their faith in Yahweh and their obedience to the law in terms of the inclusiveness of human experience – natural, historical and divine. Since all was the creation of God who had established a covenant relationship with them that covered, therefore, all their experience, nothing was excluded from their purview in the pursuit of true faithfulness. In the light of this approach, they believed that their reason was also a gift of God and could be used to discover the will of God for them. Hence Isaiah's expectation that God would invite them to reason with him. 'Come now, let us reason together, saith the Lord'.[9] To think of God and their faith in relation to their experience of the world in all its aspects required that they hold everything together because God's covenant was an expression of his creative purpose. It also meant, of course, that there could be nothing in the world that could take the place of God; to idolize the creature above the Creator was to invest in nothingness, and to put one's faith in a puff of smoke, here today and gone tomorrow. One's reason brought one to one's senses, as well as one's affection and sense of the awfulness of God's presence.

There is such a thing as 'faithful reason' for the Israelite, as there was to be later for the Christian, though they may well have different connotations.[10]

The crucial perspective with which the Israelites were dealing was the future. In a powerful sense, what we have in the Old Testament is the story, or perhaps one should say stories, by which the Israelites trace the way in which their celebration of the past in God's frequent rescue of his recalcitrant people is transformed through reflection on the nature and being of God, into an unshakeable hope for the future. This transformation could not be based on anything other than God's loving-kindness; they knew it was not their own work since they knew themselves to have been so many times disobedient. Worshipping themselves so as to make an idol of their own ambition was like any other worship of the creation as opposed to the Creator. In addition, what they saw as having its origin in a promise to themselves, they came to see as a promise to all humanity and to all creation.

Expectation and hope were not late developments in the Old Testament; on the contrary, they are rooted in the very nature of things as far as the Israelites were concerned. The very fact that God pronounced the world, his creation, to be good suggested that the future could reasonably be anticipated with optimism. And this overarching belief in the fundamental goodness of creation came as the implication of God's mighty works, which for the Israelites were acts of salvation wrought by God in history. God acting has been a category of Old Testament interpretation for years.[11] We now find the notion of God acting directly in history as problematic.[12] But what within the framework of Old Testament theology we now believe we are asked to consider, is the way in which the divine framework of creation and the careful attention of faithful humanity can bring about the purpose of God in creating. Hence the focus is on the nature and being of God.

The God of their fathers, of Abraham, of Isaac and of Jacob had declared himself to Moses in almost necessarily ambiguous terms out of the burning bush. 'I am the God of your father, the God of Abraham, the God of Isaac, and the

God of Jacob.'[13] Moses is naturally anxious about the reception he is likely to get from Pharaoh when he tells him that Yahweh commands him to release his people, Israel. God's response is not to quote a list of his successes, to draw attention to the soundness of his finances, or to say how his record in negotiations is second to none. Much more significantly Yahweh says, 'I am who I am', or as many scholars now accept, 'I shall be (with you) as I shall be (with you)'.[14] The ambiguity, if such there be, is powerfully resonant. The emphasis is not simply on the future, and the assurance that neither Moses himself nor the Israelites should be fearful of it, but on the nature of Yahweh, who is the absolute reason for and ground of their confidence. Yahweh is who Yahweh is; Yahweh will be who Yahweh will be. The Old Testament may have no explicit statement of belief in Yahweh as omnipotent, omniscient and all-loving in the precise sense that I explored in the first chapter, but one can see that they are consistent. It is Yahweh who goes before them, and will go before them; he it is in whom they can have confidence. They are partners.

Of course, they had to be reminded of this from time to time when the going got tough. The garnering of possessions may have been the reward for faith as some believed, but even if it were, to transfer trust from the Giver to the gift and to put one's faith in material things would be a snare and a delusion. Power was another temptation. The future could not be guaranteed by their own military strength, political influence, or capacity to manipulate the market – such as it was at the time. One was only as good as one's last battle, one's last negotiated settlement, or one's last business deal. Any leader would do well to reflect on this from time to time: no one can bring an end to change, remove all threat, or even defeat a local version of evil for all time. What one can always hope to do is to make some progress, to make a contribution and to go forward in partnership with God whose promise invites confident participation in the work.

In time the hope of the Israelites came to focus around the concept of messiahship. The use of the term, which means 'anointed', was not specific to start with, for it could be applied to anyone inspired by God with special functions – a priest, for example. To claim oneself to be a messiah was, of course, always bad form; messiahship was always thrust on one! In particular, if we are to understand messiahship in context it is important to keep it clear of association with Jesus' life and ministry, though as we shall see the early conversation of Christians about Jesus drew illuminatingly on themes from the messianic tradition.

The anointing of David by Samuel as king of Israel is a central feature of Israelite history, as we can see from the promise of God through Nathan, that the throne should be established for ever.[15] The prophets Isaiah and Jeremiah, in the face of military threats from Assyria and Babylon to the kingdom of Israel, looked for a future king of the house of David, and Ezekiel in exile had no doubt that the nation would be restored to Jerusalem and ruled over by God's servant David.[16] The image of the shepherd, associated with David from the beginning, continued to be an aspect of future kingly hope. And the hope remained alive; it is even found in the Qumran material where the hope may be shared between two messiahs, one royal and the other priestly. The key thing to hang on to is the continuity of the hope bound up with the nature of Yahweh as Creator of the world and Redeemer of Israel.

Putting this hope, however, alongside their frequently awful experience and consequent suffering was a demanding task. The Exodus was the supreme event in their history. Yahweh delivered his people through many signs and wonders from slavery in Egypt and brought them to the Promised Land, a land flowing with milk and honey. But they had to fight for their lives in a hostile environment, endure internal conflicts, conquest and exile. A disturbing but potentially inspiring thought began to emerge in their thinking. Was their very suffering a way in which they were living through their faithfulness to the purpose of God in creating? What were they discovering about God's purpose and their own place in it? What could they say? The house and lineage of King David was an expression of the life of the whole people of Israel; it embodied their relationship with God. The

Temple in Jerusalem was the place where Yahweh had chosen to dwell and to place his name. The exiles in Babylon were apart from both; there was no king in exile and there was no Temple. Indeed their association of Yahweh with a physical place and an inherited lineage was brought into question while at one and the same time their experience confirmed the reality of God's continuing loving-kindness. They built houses, tilled fields and grew crops, they bred and reared animals; in fact, they were able to make a living and, to their delight and amazement, they were able to worship God. What sense were they to make of this?

Already associated with the notion of kingship was the powerful image of the shepherd. Shepherding was associated with the role of kingship and also with Yahweh, as Psalm 23 testifies. 'The Lord is my shepherd; I shall not want.' The joy of the worshipper in God's temple fills him with the expectation that 'surely goodness and mercy shall follow me all the days of my life, and I shall dwell in the house of the Lord my whole life long'.[17] The transformation of representative *persona* from king through shepherd to servant is not difficult to understand since the notion of tending is common to them all. I say *persona* not person because it is not clear whether the Suffering Servant is conceived by Deutero-Isaiah as a person, as collectively the people of Israel, or as a holy remnant. Indeed, it is not clear whether the servant is to be construed as in some sense messianic or in the mythological terms of a dying and rising God. In whatever way we look at it, whether personal, collective or mythological, it seems reasonable to regard it as representative of the whole people of Israel *and*, if not actually messianic, in some significant sense a yearning for some future personal realization.

There are remarkable features implicit in the so-called servant-songs; we must now look more closely at them. The servant is innocent and without blemish. First, the sense of justice that illuminates the Israelite conception of God's loving relationship with Israel means that he cannot be held to be suffering on his own behalf in order to expiate his own sins. He suffers, as the prophet makes clear, for rebellious sinners on behalf of whom he intercedes and by whose sacrifice their stripes would be healed. But who are these people really? Moreover, second, he was called to his awful responsibility by Yahweh from whom he willingly accepted it. What does this say of Yahweh, who has a covenant relationship with Israel? Third, the servant does not attract concern or interest when he delivers the word of God; he was not listened to. He was 'despised and rejected of men', so that he had no compensating sense of fulfilling an important role that would eventually lead to public recognition. What he suffered, he suffered in humiliating loneliness and obscurity with the consequence that he was buried not with the redeemed, but with the wicked and rebellious. Fourth, he suffered not simply on behalf of his people, the Israelites, but announced Yahweh's salvation to the end of the earth. What does this say about the sense that the Israelites had of being special, of being God's chosen people? And, fifth, he undertook all this in obedience to Yahweh's word in full confidence of Yahweh's promise that his suffering would bring justification to many, and that his recompense would be with God.[18]

The implications are breathtaking. Yahweh is certainly Creator and Redeemer, but as such he not only leads, he suffers with his people. The choosing of Israel is for the entire world, not simply for them. They will fulfil their role, despite their disobedience and failures. They have a future because it is in God's hands, not theirs; above all, their hope, and the hope of the whole world, lies with Yahweh who has been a conversation partner with Israel through her history. When she has been attentive and willing to work at her role she has been overcome by the grace of God's loving-kindness. Israel's history is hugely and, mercifully for all our sakes, a matter of learning to hope. It depends for its fulfilment and for its learning potential on the emergence of the strength and courage to suffer for the sake of the world and for its salvation. The privilege that the Israelites share as a result of the calling of Yahweh and their election as God's chosen people is not that they are chosen to save themselves, but chosen so that the world through their experience might come to know the presence of the Living God. This terrifying burden is paradoxically not unbearable because it is shared with God, in conversation with whom they work out what it is to live faithfully and hopefully.

One other Old Testament image can inspire further reflection: the Son of Man. As time went on, the disappointment following the excitement of the return from exile in Babylon led the Israelites to centre their hope upon direct revelation and divine intervention. Faith in God was essential, but clearly their future was outside their influence, apart from the attempt to discern the true meaning of the law and be obedient to it. The role of the Jews was in principle passive. This apocalyptic dimension had been a minor feature of the prophetic tradition from the beginning, but it now began to take over, as one can see, for example, in the books of Daniel and 1 and 2 Enoch. The Jews faced further persecution in the second and first centuries BC, and believed their only hope was in God. As the book of Daniel has it, 'one like unto a Son of Man' (AV) presents himself to the Ancient of Days, who gives him 'dominion, and glory and kingship, that all peoples, nations, and languages should serve him; his dominion is an everlasting dominion that shall not pass away, and his kingship is one that shall never be destroyed'.[19] The Son of Man seems to be neither human nor divine, but some heavenly prince of Israel who brings salvation and destroys the beasts of hell. In Enoch, the image is associated with a messianic king who will establish a theocratic kingdom of peace and prosperity.

Later traditions of Judaism will make much of this apocalyptic imagery, though this further period of reflection and conversation, while not inconsistent with what has gone before, is far from being a development of the whole tradition. For mainstream Judaism and for one strand of thinking, the Christian which emerges in association with it, discussion and enquiry continue to embrace the most significant frameworks of personal reflection, history and creation. Neither Jew nor Christian is concerned to get out of the world, to try to think apart from it, or to ignore it: we are both peoples of the earth led to share in the human discussion across the generations. History and the natural world are alike aspects of God's creative purpose. Attention to them is essential if we are to understand the school of faith in which we are learning to hope.

Jesus stands firmly in that broad tradition.

3

The Jesus Community:
A New Conversation?

So who was this fellow Jesus? It's a good question: the range of answers scholars have proposed is considerable. The most important fact to hold on to from our point of view is that he was a Jew, born into the Jewish tradition. He was, as far as we can see, familiar with the Old Testament scriptures and no doubt with much other material, oral and perhaps written, that he unconsciously absorbed as he grew up in and contributed to the conversation of a normal Jewish family.

I say 'normal Jewish family', but surely the New Testament makes it clear that his family was anything but normal. No man who is said to have been born of a virgin can surely be called normal, can he? And there are several features of his family's life and his earliest experiences, at least as the Gospels present them, that indicate a string of the most extraordinary and implausible events. Let's mention a few of them.

The census under Caesar Augustus is as ordinary as anything could be. We have plenty of evidence of good bureaucratic Roman administration. The authorities would clearly want to know what the opportunities for taxation were, since the empire depended for its security upon an army that had to be paid. This would be especially important in occupied territory, and a census would provide much-needed evidence. The first general census in Britain did not occur until 1841, but the Roman empire was astonishingly well governed! But then we come to other stories connected with the birth of Jesus. What do you make of the announcement of 'good tidings of great joy' by the angel Gabriel to astonished shepherds, and the alleged arrival on time of the angelic host with an anthem? And how do even the wisest of Wise Men follow a star so accurately all the way across the desert to Bethlehem, carrying gold, frankincense and myrrh? How do they with such uncanny precision identify exactly the stable of the very inn where Mary had given birth to Jesus? Who stopped the star over where the young child lay and for how long? Why didn't everything else stop as well? Warnings of Herod's jealousy, fear and anger are revealed to Joseph in a dream and he sets off, according to Matthew, with his new family to Egypt where he remains until after Herod's death.

Huge tomes have been written about these stories exploring their meaning by researching their origins, historicity and mythological significance; we could spend the rest of this book exploring them. I do not for one moment wish to suggest that this would necessarily be pointless: all such scholarship can be profitable in one way or another. However, for our present purpose it is only necessary to underline one matter which is nevertheless of vital importance. Jesus, having been introduced to the conversation of the generations in the family of Judaism, continues the conversation of his people with God; he does not begin a new one. What is more, the birth narratives, written after the death and resurrection of Jesus, reflect the familiarity of all the writers of the Gospels with the conversation of the Jewish tradition; they place Jesus firmly in that framework.

The stories push us too, therefore, into a position where we have to recognize that we shall make no sense of the meaning of Jesus' life if we think that with him we begin a new story. We do not: we are not left fishing around for a context in which to place him. If we are to understand Jesus, we have to see him in the continuity of the traditions of the Old Testament, to which we have already given some attention.

It is not, of course, the case that the Old Testament alone provides us with everything that we shall need, for as we found with the complex influences on the Jewish tradition itself, the Christian experience of life has to be brought into relationship with the many other traditions to be found in the conversation of the generations. These will include, for example, not only Greek, Roman, Persian and Hellenistic approaches to life's meaning, but the nourishing consequences of bringing the theological enquiry aroused by reflection upon the life and work of Jesus into conversation with historians, literary scholars, astronomers, cosmologists, geneticists, psychologists, and so on. For ever! The Christian tradition is not simply a fulfilment of Jewish prophecy, which is why at the close of the previous chapter I referred to it as growing up *in association* with Judaism; it is, of course, highly indebted to Judaism and should never forget the fact, but it cannot be explained, or therefore lived out, in terms of Judaism alone.

We don't, as a matter a fact, know much about Jesus' life – the carpenter's shop and all that – so let's begin towards the end of Jesus' life with his ministry, which it is argued lasted no more than three years and perhaps only one. Of one thing we can be sure – whatever the circumstances of Jesus' birth and early life, Jesus was an attractive figure whose wandering ministry stimulated tremendous interest and local excitement. He enjoyed company and was regarded as rather entertaining. He drew to himself a disparate group of followers but also came to be regarded by the authorities as a threat to the established order, whether seen from a Jewish or Roman perspective. Palestine was a minor colony of the Roman empire within which a mélange of cultures, languages, religious practices, traditions and philosophies struggled for dominance. In one sense the Roman authorities could not have cared less what went on as long as taxes were paid, but any threat to public order naturally attracted their interest since it could involve military intervention and imperial expense. And as far as the Jewish authorities were concerned, any disturbance of the peace, especially if it appeared to them to misinterpret their own history and expectation and therefore to challenge their authority, had to be nipped in the bud. If they were not seen to act against potential revolt, they would be in trouble from their own people, let alone the Romans. As things stood, Judaism was a *religio licita* in the Roman empire, that is, a permitted religion which, given the declared position of the emperor as a divine figure, meant they had a delicate path to tread.

Within his own Jewish community, as we have seen, many of Jesus' compatriots had for generations been learning to hope for a divinely inaugurated future kingdom of happiness and peace, but this living expectation of imminent salvation ran alongside a realistic appreciation that it would not all be plain sailing. Some renegades from time to time seem to have confused religious enthusiasm with political aspiration: they treated unusual events as signs and fomented unrest in the hope that religious fervour would not only initiate the intervention of divine power to establish the messianic kingdom, but also lead to the expulsion of the Roman forces. But how would one recognize when things were beginning to move in the right direction?

It's a bit like arguing about the economy. The same sign can indicate both success and potential difficulty. What are the signs of a successful economy? Increased trade between the nations, higher employment, better wages and reduction in poverty, improving profits and a reduction in debt, care of the environment, and so on? I suppose most of us would think these relevant features and want something of each. But then, some of the signs of success can have a deleterious effect. Higher employment means pressure on wage rates, which means lower investment, which means less research and development, which means fewer new products, which means lower employment. Or is your preferred sign of economic success the annual double-digit growth that the Chinese and potentially the Indian economies enjoy at the moment? But rapid growth in such huge economies means increases in world commodity and energy prices and cheap goods flooding the market because of low wages, which while initially bringing about a rise in stock market values, will put pressure on production in developed western and Japanese economies, threaten the environment, cause unemployment, put up government costs and therefore taxes. The same signs can give contrary indications, dependent on the context and the timescale.

So what about the signs of the kingdom? Any sign that reminds people of what they have learned to hope for may, in the current moral and political crisis of first-century Palestine, also be a threat to authority. So it was when, as Mark has it, Jesus comes announcing the inauguration of the kingdom of God. What were people to make of it, especially when it seems his first task is to recruit disciples? How are they to think about it? Are they genuinely members of Rabbi Jesus' school, or are they potential ministers of state in the new kingdom of God? What's it all about?

We know little about the disciples, who were interested in Jesus' teaching, even those few who accompanied him. Clearly there must have been several rings of discipleship. There would be those who heard him as he passed through their village and were attracted by what he said and did; but the majority would have remained at home with their families, on their farms, in their offices and workshops, reminiscing about it, chatting every now and again with friends and neighbours about what it all meant. They would have remembered particularly stories and events that related to their particular trade or vocation. Their interest would be stirred up again in the light of the later events of the Passion and the subsequent rumours that spread abroad about the subsequent marvels of resurrection and ascension. Then there was the smaller number who left home and followed him from time to time, utterly astonished by what he was saying and on the edge of their seats, as it were, wondering what would happen next. They wanted to be in on the act, if there was one!

Only then should we think of that very small number, those perhaps whom we know as 'the disciples', who actually committed themselves to him and joined him as a sort of travelling school. They wanted to talk it out with him, not just among themselves or on their own account in the light of the tradition that in itself, while providing important dimensions of constructive conversation, did not satisfy them. They were not just impressed by him, they were over-whelmed, that is by Jesus himself, his personality, his character, his sensitivity, his forthrightness and perhaps above all by his sheer presence. He invited questions of himself, 'Who do they say that I am?' Apparently, in his own remarks about his own person he alluded beyond himself to his Father, to God. What *on earth* (I use the phrase advisedly) did that amount to?

The kingdom that Jesus announced was now upon them, he affirmed. Scholars talk of this as 'realized eschatology' – the beginning of the end – and I want to stick with that scholarly term for a moment. We often refer to some event retrospectively and say, 'I never realized at the time what was going on'. For example, suppose a friend invites you to lunch. You turn up and find he's invited another person, the vice-chancellor of a neighbouring university. The restaurant is superb and the conversation rather good. Indeed, you find her a most interesting person perhaps because she seems to be very interested in your own research.

Some six months later, a headhunter telephones to call your attention to the fact that the Pirenne Chair in Medieval History is advertised. You had noticed it but decided that you were too young to apply. The headhunter invites you to meet him and you decide to apply after all; nothing ventured, nothing won, you think. The interviews go well; the final one is chaired by the vice-chancellor whom you recognize. To your surprise and pleasure you are appointed. Some time later you meet the vice-chancellor again. She reminds you of the lunch and says that she had set the whole thing up because your name had been drawn to her attention as an up-and-coming scholar and she had to find the right person for the important Pirenne Chair. She had been impressed and asked the headhunter to approach you. You had not realized it at the time but the next stage of your life was already taking shape. Think analogously of 'realized eschatology'; it's a doctrine of 'the next things' rather than 'a doctrine of the last things' – except in so far as 'the last things' include all those things that contribute to their progressive realization along the way.

What Jesus realized was that the kingdom that the Jews – indeed all humankind, and the whole creation – want and wait for with varying degrees of patience was here already; it had been established by God in his creating. God had taken the waiting out of wanting, right at the beginning. It could not be otherwise since, as the Jews celebrated only too well in their traditions about the Passover, the God of their salvation, who had brought them out of Egypt and given them as a sign to the whole of humankind, was also the God of all creation who in creating had committed himself to the success of all that he had set his mind on. Nothing could be plainer – to Jesus! God is present with his world; so there could be peace on earth among all people of good will. His mission, Jesus believed, was to make what was plain to him plain to others, beginning with his own people, but not focused exclusively upon them.

So I take Jesus' miracles to be occasions when it dawned on all concerned that whatever was going on revealed the living presence and power of God in God's world.[1] The exciting thing about this approach is that almost any event whatsoever can legitimately be regarded as miraculous if it gives rise to a realization of God's active partnership with his people in bringing about the successful fulfilment of his purpose in creating. Dunkirk, the discovery of penicillin, stem cell research,[2] W. G. Sebald's novels, Chekhov's plays, Plato's *Republic*, Bach's 48 Preludes and Fugues, Egon Schiele's paintings, and fine specimens of the culture of the *liliacae* family would be just a few of my examples. What would you want to add? It would be interesting to discuss our respective criteria, why we thought our choices were truly revelatory, and what we meant by 'revelatory'.

The stories of Jesus, which we usually call parables, are also occasions when their successful telling leads to an analogous insight. 'So that's what it's all about!' we say, as we are drawn into the action of the story; or, as I. T. Ramsey said of religious language as a whole, when we are awaked from our moral and intellectual slumber and 'the penny drops'.[3] Luke reports Jesus telling what I think of as the Boy Scout motto: Be prepared! 'Since it is your Father's pleasure to give you the kingdom,' Luke reports Jesus as saying, 'have confidence to live your life in the light of that fact; so doing will bring the kingdom nearer. That might involve you in giving away your possessions, but it will paradoxically be an investment, so get on with it.' There is clearly not a little concern on the part of Peter and others who are present. 'Okay,' they say, 'but it doesn't always look as if the promise of God, which of course we're sure we can trust, is going to happen any time soon, so hadn't we better take precautions?' 'Sure,' says Jesus, 'but don't let your proper carefulness degenerate into complacency or you will simply not recognize the signs when they occur. Don't forget it is happening now, if only you would realize it,' by which he means, 'Make a reality of it in your lives, the way you live with one another now in God's good world. The future is in our hands.' It is so easy to miss opportunities, as the parable of the talents underlines: only two of them traded, the third played safe and missed the point.

Jesus copes with misunderstanding brilliantly, often with generous humour and often in connection with a miracle. Matthew reports that a blind and dumb demoniac was brought to Jesus and was healed.[4] The people were amazed (who wouldn't be!), and the Pharisees are angry. Well, the Pharisees know according to their own teaching that the man's disabilities are the result of his sins or those of his forebears, so they must be the consequence of just divine retribution. Who does this man Jesus think he is, challenging God's judgement? They could not deny the evidence of their eyes and retain the respect of the crowd for the man was evidently healed; so they say it must be a trick of Beelzebub, the Devil (the Lord of the Flies) who has possessed Jesus with his power. Only the Senior Devil could have power over junior devils, as C. S. Lewis recognized in *The Screwtape Letters*, so since it could not be God whose power Jesus had called upon, it must be Satan's.[5] But, as Jesus sees it, the kingdom is here and Jesus has to make that plain to all. So he says, 'Fine, you're right, let's say that I have done this by Satan's power. Surely that's an occasion for rejoicing, for it means that there's civil war in hell, and no kingdom divided against itself can survive. Cheer up, then; the Devil is on the way to extinction! On the other hand, just suppose for a moment that I am acting in the name and with the power of God, what would you say then? Surely, you would see that the Kingdom is upon us!' They didn't, apparently.

Again and again Jesus hammers this home in the face of anxiety, intelligent questioning, fear and suspicion. He insists in word and action that the kingdom of God is here *and* will be established with power for ever. Jesus moves about the countryside, through villages addressing large crowds, talking with an individual woman, embracing children, having supper with a tax gatherer, restoring health to many who suffer, trying to open minds and hearts to an awareness of the presence of the Living God, the Father of everything in heaven and on earth.

The miracles and parables alike are dedicated to this purpose. When asked by his confused disciples what it means, Jesus explains the parable of the sower. 'Yes, of course not everything looks perfect at the moment, but just look at what fertile ground can produce with the good seed of God's word – and you are all potentially fertile ground!' He offers the encouragement of the parable of the two sons. 'Don't write yourselves off and think that there is a simple choice between staying at home and being prissy about it, or asking for your inheritance and going on a world tour. Neither offers a secure way forward. Your future is in your own hands because that is where God has put it; the kingdom is yours!' But the message doesn't seem to get across.

Not even the disciples seem to get the point. Actually they are, not surprisingly, just like the rest of the community of whom they are a part anyway – a point the truth of which the leaders and teachers of the Church need to be reminded of from time to time! For example, they share the accepted view about the origin of disability. They are prompted to ask Jesus a question when they see a man blind from birth: 'Rabbi, who sinned, this man or his parents that he was born blind?' It's a natural question, since although the tradition accepted that the sins of the fathers would be visited on the children – a view that politicians and others would do well to remember today when choosing policies! – if a person is blind from birth there does seem to be some injustice. As far as Jesus and God's kingdom are concerned, that is beside the point. So

Jesus replies, 'Neither! Of course it is not God's will that a person be blind, God's kingdom is quite independent of whether a person is blind or is sighted. The blind too can enter the kingdom.'

Jesus does his best to show them what is really going on in God's world in everything he says and does. 'It's happening now all around you, look at the sparrows and the lilies of the field,' he urges them. And yet, the disciples are all of a dither: they swing from excitement to depression, optimism to despondency. Is he the one who is to come? Is he the messiah? Is he ever going to declare himself, get going and make it plain for all to see? They are puzzled; they argue, quarrel and embrace doubt, faith and despair. Just like us, really. But, paradoxically, they continue on balance to retain their hope.

Their hope centres on their experience of Jesus as a person as much as it does on his actions and his words. The words they hear him speak and the actions they see him perform are not separate from their experience of him, of course, but it is the doer and the speaker who fascinates and excites him, rather than the actions and words themselves. He is simply the most extraordinary person they have ever come across. As the Gospels suggest, he has an air of authority; even evil spirits fall at his word – in other words they see him conquering evil in its most naked form. Those stories of the temptations in which Satan fails to seduce him with his blandishments ring true.

Sometimes the disciples misunderstand even the nature of the kingdom; they talk and think of it in terms of power and wealth as if they believed the fruit of the Spirit was cash and cakes. In feeding the five thousand Jesus announced nourishment for all in God's good world – if you really want it! Yet in the face of such dramatic optimism and confidence in God, they yet again failed to see the light. Some commentators, for example, set the scene for their misunderstanding in this way. They suggest that it was yet another occasion when the disciples jumped to the wrong conclusion; the kingdom they expected was just around the corner and the crowd constituted the accompanying military power.[6] The crowd was probably in on it too. Who would want to go into the desert, even following a charismatic personality like Jesus, unless they were anticipating some excitement! There is apparent supporting evidence in Mark. The crowd consists only of men; they were drawn up in military formation, fifties and hundreds. Moreover, it was at the time of the Passover, as is evident from the flowers blooming in the desert, and that was when the messiah was expected. Jesus' reaction is to go away calmly by himself in case the crowd – led perhaps by the disciples? – tries to push him into premature and utterly misleading activity. Jesus is not in their pocket or in anyone's power, he lives in God's loving presence.[7]

John sets the miracle of feeding in a much larger framework of power, God's creative power over nature. On the following day the no doubt disappointed and puzzled disciples cross the lake in a boat. The disciples 'see' Jesus walking to them on the water in a storm. (I wonder what exactly 'see' means here; any ideas?) The Jews feared the sea, with which they were much less familiar than were other peoples of the Mediterranean littoral, such as the Greeks; it was for them the habitation of the Leviathan, a wild environment possessed of unknown evil. Freud found the sea a useful image of the unconscious. The unconscious, like the sea, may harbour the wrecks of past experience and all sorts of threat, the shocking memory of which may be suddenly aroused by new events to disturb our equilibrium. But, John insists, Jesus with God's authority is master of the winds and the waves. The whole experience provides Jesus with the opportunity to get across yet again the fact of God's presence with his world and, above all, the importance of understanding that the real purpose of food is to provide nourishment for the discernment of the Father. 'I am the bread that came down from heaven.'[8] The food, this manna, is available for all, and so is God; there is nothing to fear.

The illusory kingdom-expectations of the disciples are the product of their own anxieties and fears. In the absence of confirmation of their mistaken hopes, they look to their own strength to bring them about. In so doing they therefore become jealous of one another. Who is the favourite? Who

will inherit? Which of them will be in power in the new kingdom? What can they do to bring things to a head?

There is nothing more disturbing than being constantly
misunderstood; Jesus must have felt this keenly. Indeed, on
the way up to Jerusalem Luke indicates that Jesus wept over
the city and its symbolic failure to accept the implications of
God's promises to Israel. What was he to do? He was already
trying to express in his person nothing but a sign of the
loving presence of God but he came to believe that the only
way that he could get the message across was to *give* himself
to it absolutely. And having come to this opinion, he believed
also that this was God's will for him, for everybody's sake.
Some say that this was always in his mind because it was what
God had intended from the beginning. I think this unlikely
because Jesus himself, like every other member of the human
race, was also learning to hope, and finding out on a day-by-
day basis what this means. Since all learning implies sharing
experience, what Jesus is anxious to do in his own living and
teaching is to participate in and develop the conversation that
God has with the world from the beginning, and to involve
humankind in it. If in his acceptance of his sacrifice he could
present this perfectly on behalf of everyone perhaps humankind, finding itself implicitly included in the conversation,
will want to know what it means, and how to live it out for
itself in word and action. And so it has proved. But it did
involve Jesus in seeing it through to the bitter end, in his death.

The writers of the Gospels take a third of their space in
covering this most crucial termination of Jesus' life; for Jesus
it was no more than a week. So in space and time, the revelation of the world's meaning is focused upon the confined
countryside of Palestine, a minor province of the Roman
empire, and the three years, ultimately concentrated into just
a final week of one man's lonely public ministry. In that
meagre space and time, Jesus discovered the wonders of
God's creative energy, the richness and fertility of God's
world, its generosity and promise, and also the fine character
– potentially – of humankind to whom in the community of
the people of Israel on behalf of all humankind, God had
committed God's self.

The sadness and perplexity aroused in the heart of Jesus by this unrealized potential, despite its real presence, cannot even be imagined. Any teacher or parent will perhaps be dimly aware of something like it observing a group of bright pupils dissipate their energies, misapply their talents, flaunt discipline, reject proffered affectionate support, and disappear into the dark hinterland of illiteracy, incompetence and drug-infected crime, secure in their own self-righteous vision. To try in such circumstances to keep alive the thought that they still have potential – which they have – is indeed to enter a tough school, where one may nevertheless 'learn to hope'. For Jesus, apparently, it involves 'setting his face towards Jerusalem' and accepting the judgement of the world and apparent failure, in the hope that God will overcome the world.

He asks that preparations be made for the Passover, but somehow the message gets out – 'He's coming! Jesus is coming to Jerusalem for the feast of the Passover.' All hell is let loose! Crowds in the street, palm branches, cheering, singing, marching. And then panic on the part of the authorities. What now? Their worst fears are aroused. The chief priests and their allies want to make it quite clear to the Romans and to the people that this 'king' is a renegade, certainly not one of them. The Roman governor is concerned above all to keep law and order. The best thing for them to do is to work together to arrest Jesus and get him out of the way on one pretext or another. Charging him with threatening the temple seems a good line for the Jewish religious authorities to take, and if that can be attached to the blasphemy of claiming the title of king so that the Romans can treat it as attempted insurrection, so much the better. And so it is. Jesus says what he is about, and what he believes God is about, with his life.

The outcome is very pleasing for the high priests and for the Roman governor. They must have been delighted to get away with it; they thought there might have been real trouble, but in the event it all passed off quite peacefully. Judas, one of the inner circle of disciples, is said to have betrayed him and Peter to have drawn a sword in his defence.

Both misunderstood to the very end what Jesus was about. Judas may have been one of those who thought he could force the pace, and the bold Peter may even have believed that the end was beginning; all that was needed was this final push and everything would be revealed. But Judas took his own life when things worked out differently; he had loved Jesus too and in his desperate remorse could not forgive himself. And Peter was disillusioned when Jesus told him to put up his sword, so disillusioned indeed that when, as the tradition has it, he was accused later by a serving maid in the pub that he was one of them, he denied it. He was not going to be on the losing side.

In the meantime, there had been the mysterious nature of Jesus' last meal with his disciples, his arrest in Gethsemane, his trial(s), Jesus' awful death by crucifixion and his reported stunning last words from the cross to a dying criminal, 'Today, you will be with me in Paradise'. I say 'in the mean-time' since one might have thought that these events would be no more than footnotes in history, trivial things that happened while all that really affected the future of the world went on anyway. Latter-day scribblers interested in the minutiae of local affairs might have produced an article or two for *The Mystical Times*, but no more. After all, everyone knows what the world of human life is really about, including the great world of the Roman empire!

What matters are wars and battles, policy decisions, inter-national meetings, decisions about taxation, the accumula-tion of wealth, the patronage of next year's games with all the menagerie of wild animals to be brought from North Africa for slaughter in the Colosseum, the securing of food supplies for the inhabitants of that great city, and the recruit-ment and training of the army, etc., etc. But not so. The Roman empire has gone – its emperors, generals, wealth and power, its military prowess destroyed; there survives only its law, its administrative system (largely in the Roman Catholic Church), its road system and central heating. And Jesus? His influence lives and grows. Indeed, we Christians have learned to hope because we say not that his influence survives, but 'Jesus lives!' He learned to hope and by his conversation and ultimate sacrifice communicated that hope to others. Can we, dare we, take up the conversation in our own time, and learn to hope? The challenge is just as great for us now when the world's affairs weigh just as heavily on us as they did on the disciples and the people of first-century Palestine.

It is one of the most intriguing aspects of the whole story as we find it in the Gospels: there were 'disciples' who just could not give up thinking and talking about Jesus. He may have died, been treated as a criminal and put to death in a horrible way but many people in small groups in the villages through which he had travelled on his journey to Jerusalem, where he had told stories, wrought miracles and 'preached the gospel', continued to think, reflect and question what it was all about. Was it about anything at all? Did it matter?

Well, they stood in traditions of interpretation that gave them some frameworks of conversation with which to explore their experience of Jesus. They could not give up: they were still attracted to Jesus. In their societies the farmers, carpenters, workmen, Greeks as well as Jews, and soon Romans as well as Jews and Greeks, felt themselves involved with something vital, indeed with someone whose death was strangely life-giving. Their despair turned into expectation as their conversation caught fire and transformed their growing understanding into infectious hope. Hope was not something they were waiting any longer for someone to bring, it was the foundation of what they could actually do now to realize the future that Jesus had offered them in his life and confirmed in his death. Here is genuine 'realized eschatology'; the kingdom is established and nothing will stand in its way. We hope to learn the same truth so that we too will learn to hope.

This is certainly no new conversation, but the continuation of the conversation between the generations that I shall explore in the next chapter.

4

The Community of Faith:
What Can We Say?

I remarked in the previous chapter that we know singularly little of the details about the actual life of Jesus. Fortunately we know somewhat more about the subsequent development of the conversation he had with his disciples and the consequent establishment of what we now know as 'the Church'. There were many groups who kept his memory alive and were intrigued to develop a narrative that did justice to his story. In what context could they set his life and what they wanted to say about him so as to get a purchase on his significance? To which, if any, of the many traditions of Judaism could he be related so as to build a narrative to support what the growing numbers of 'followers' were beginning to want to say about him? Was he best thought of as a prophet, priest or king? Or what about those other dimensions in their tradition – Son of Man, Suffering Servant or, most daring of all, Christ, even Son of God? Their minds were alive with amazement, excitement, delight, dread and hope. Reading the books of the New Testament enables us to share the quickened interest and confusion that arose from their overwhelming sense of having been, *and of being*, in the presence of someone who had transformed their hopes.

This seems to have been the nub of the matter. Those who had been involved with Jesus simply couldn't get him out of their heads. The stories and miracles of Jesus were important; they carried a message, didn't they? At any rate, the stories were kept alive by being retold in more than one small group. This is clear from the fact that we have more than one source of some of them, such as the feeding of the multitudes that is actually told twice in the Gospel of Mark, and in different forms. On the other hand, individual stories crop up uniquely in only one of the Gospels. The same is true of the miracles; they lived on in the telling because Jesus' miracles remained good stories whenever they were remembered, whether they were in fact miraculous or not.

The end of the Roman republic and the beginning of the empire was a century of moral perplexity, a clash of philosophies and religious anxiety. The more we know about it the more unsurprising it is that we come across plenty of evidence that miracle-workers and storytellers abounded. Jesus would not have been conspicuous simply through his good stories and reported actions. We know only too well from our own current experience that lack of moral coherence and shared philosophical perspective allows go-getters, soothsayers, charlatans, fundamentalist nonsense and mumbo-jumbo to flourish. It's the money that counts! So what is it about Jesus that made him so vitally memorable to so many people?

It seems clear that what caused him to be talked about and made what he had to say unforgettable was the sheer impact of Jesus the man. It was Jesus himself and the manner of his death that raised the real questions for those who met him and those who followed in later generations. Of course, the parables and miracles of Jesus warrant attention for they are intriguing in themselves, but only because of the sheer character and quality of the person of Jesus himself. Given the time, such stories and miracles are two a penny. No, it's not the stories and miracles, it is the questions raised by Jesus about his own person that point to the real issues raised for the disciples. What the disciples see and hear arouses a consuming interest in who Jesus is and stimulates their active reflection on the meaning not only of his life, but of their lives. He is no ordinary storyteller and miracle-worker.

And, intriguingly, it is their experience of Jesus the man himself that leads them directly towards serious theological enquiry, not mere idle speculation. That's what it's all about, serious *theological* enquiry. Jesus seems to know such a lot about God, indeed seems to know God intimately. Suppose he does know things that they did not know, suppose he really does know God! The disciples must have discussed it often among themselves.

> 'If Jesus does know God then what does that have to teach us about the nature of God?'
> 'And about the world and ourselves?'
> 'Yes, and what does that say about *him*? Who is he?'

The amusing story that Jesus told the scribes when he was accused of casting out demons by calling on Beelzebub must surely have come to mind. 'Okay,' said Jesus, 'you're right. But if that's the case then there's civil war in hell, so cheer up! But what if I speak with God's authority? What then?' The disciples will have wrestled with the question. We will too, if we are wise.

Jesus put the question to them directly: 'Who do people say that I am?'[1] If this is the question that faced the disciples, it is also the question that has, I believe, concerned Christians throughout the ages. It is a very searching question. Consideration of it led the writers of the Gospels to focus on the events surrounding Jesus' death; about a third of each Gospel concerns the last week of Jesus' life and the stories that circulated about his 'resurrection' remarkably quickly afterwards. It often seems to me that we have become so used to the stories of the resurrection that the sheer shock of them escapes us. The disciples were not completely stupid; and it was, moreover, a thought utterly outside their ordinary Jewish traditions. At the very least the experience of the disciples before and after the death of Jesus kept the issue alive in their minds: 'Who is this man?'

The debate about Jesus that first involved a small community of disciples with a Jewish rabbi is brought together in the universal conversation of the people of God, which we know as the Church. The Church is a truly astonishing worldwide organization, the most successful in history, despite all its vicissitudes. If you worship in a small congregation of a dozen or so with an average age of 70 in a village chapel where the surrounding community seem oblivious or even hostile to its existence, you might well fail to see that you are part of the realized eschatology of the kingdom of God. The mystery of Jesus, the essential power of the questions about the nature of the world and human life he posed and the astonishing success of Christianity may have little reality in the face of peeling paint and another terrible sermon. The kingdom may seem inconsistent with current experience – the offering is dwindling, expenses are growing, and the likelihood of closure looms on the horizon. But the plain astonishing fact is that it is so; real things happen here. The survival of the building is irrelevant.

Look where the Church is now. Once there were only twelve disciples – well, okay, we don't know that for certain, but it was not many! They were a motley bunch, at one another's throats half the time. Now no country lacks a Christian congregation; indeed, as is the case with the number of scientists, there are more Christians alive now than have existed before in the whole history of the world.[2] And the cultural influence is profound. Christians, for example, still calculate the date from the supposed date of Jesus' birth by referring to 2006 AD – *anno domini*, 'the year of Our Lord' – notwithstanding the growing current fashion to say 2006 CE, meaning 'Common Era' not, as some seem to think, 'Christian Era'.[3] And all this because of what Christians have come to believe about Jesus, not because he was a good storyteller or because they believe he was a jolly useful person to have at a wedding party.

This has not come about by accident; it is only because the community of faith has throughout its history tried to tease out what 'the faith' means by working at what it thinks it knows and by so doing, learning to hope. Bonhoeffer's question is useful: 'Who is Jesus Christ for us today?' Christians in communities large and small have kept alive the conversation about Jesus (we might say, 'with Jesus'), speculated about his nature, found it impossible to separate talk about Jesus from talk about God, and found it increasingly exciting to put together all this alongside all the other expressions of and feelings for human knowledge and experience of the world in the attempt to develop an understanding of God,

Creator, Redeemer, Participating Encourager – Father, Son and Holy Spirit. This is a mind-blowing claim, I appreciate, but if what Christians believe is on the right lines, then there is sufficient truth in it to make it worthwhile continuing to work at it. In human terms we can hope for nothing better – progress, not final solutions.

After all, there are no final solutions; final solutions wreak death, they do not bring life. We should know better than to set our hearts on 'final solutions' after the foul totalitarians of the twentieth century, Stalin and communism, Hitler and fascism, the barbarities of Idi Amin, Pol Pot, the butchers of Rwanda and all the rest. Christians are learning to hope; they are engaged in the pursuit of wisdom, not seeking knowledge in order to grasp at selfish power. If indeed Jesus is the Christ, the Anointed One, the Saviour of the world, the Son of God, it is because he interiorized everything that he learned in his person; he eschewed every seductive offer of a quick solution, every short cut to an illusory authority and focused on the wisdom that came from 'wanting God'. He expressed in himself everything that he believed about God and God's relationship with the world.

No point then for Jesus in paying attention to the offer of the devil from the pinnacle of the temple in Jerusalem. The Synoptic Gospels are clear about this and it is a major insight. According to Luke, for example, the devil said, 'If you are the Son of God, throw yourself down from here; for it is written, "He will command his angels concerning you, to protect you," and "On their hands they will bear you up, so that you will not dash your foot against a stone."' And Jesus answered him, 'It is said, do not put the Lord your God to the test.'[4] The devil is irrelevant to Jesus' work, for as Jesus perceives creation the devil has neither power nor authority over anything or anybody, neither on earth nor in heaven. Power and authority belong to God alone. God has power over himself and full knowledge of himself and therefore he alone is free to encourage the flourishing of everything that is other than himself by giving himself to it in loving, encouraging, participatory presence.

But it's especially interesting, don't you think, that as Luke saw it not even for Jesus was there a final solution? For Jesus as for us there is no ultimate proof in this life. As Luke says, there was always the possibility of another more opportune time. 'And when the devil had finished every test, he departed from him until an opportune time.'[5] 'An opportune time', says Luke, perhaps setting the stage for those parables in which Jesus urged his listeners 'to watch and pray' and not to become complacent or overconfident. Jesus learned that what he wanted was 'God': he wanted him to the end and in so doing gave his life for the world. He had learned to hope. He understood that his and the world's only hope, ultimately, is in God. And he lived out his belief in his death, in the words put into his mouth by Luke and John when he was on the cross, 'Father, into your hands I commit my spirit!'[6] 'It is finished!'[7]

It is impossible to say where these inspiring thoughts began. The New Testament represents a century of conversation about it among the community of faith. The Gospels are not biographies; each represents a theological reflection on the life of Jesus focusing on the last week or so of his life, supported by miracle stories, parables, confrontations with authority and faithful questioning. The earliest Gospel, Mark, may date from about 60 AD, the latest, John, from about the end of the first century. They embrace contrasting but mutually supportive theological perspectives, drawing on oral and perhaps even some written material.

The rest of the New Testament is made up of diverse texts. There are the letters of Paul, who was unacquainted with Jesus but transfixed by his 'real presence'. They were written to Christians to encourage, admonish and remind them of the basis of their faith. Some of the epistles have claims to authenticity, such as the epistles to the Galatians and to the Romans; others are attributed, such as Ephesians, but they all provide evidence for the existence of communities of faith soon after the death of Jesus. And they are brutally honest: 'If for this life only we have hoped in Christ, we are of all people most to be pitied.'[8] That is, we celebrate something real, a real presence that confirms the promise of God in creation; if not, we share in an illusion. Hope is not just a future prospect, but also, when well founded, the beginning of its realization in present experience. There is other epistolary material, such as James, Jude and John, and the final puzzling book of Revelation.

The important thing for our purpose is to appreciate the vast diversity of idea, theory, faith commitment and language that contributes to this whole complex but coherent volume we know as the New Testament. If you read it, you will discover it to be so, and be amazed. Moreover, because the 'New' Testament was inseparable in the minds of Christians from the 'Old' Testament the two were placed alongside each other in one Christian volume, the Bible. The complete list of Old and New Testament books is first affirmed by Athanasius, but perhaps not officially approved until a Council at Rome in AD 382.[9] It is the living product of the Church that fixed the canon of scripture over the course of four centuries.

As one shares in the conversation of the community of faith by reading the New Testament one becomes aware that the community itself believed that the conversation it continued with Jesus was with God. No other explanation satisfied them. Indeed it believed itself to have been called into existence by God. This is understandable given the context. The disciples were a frightened, disillusioned community, following the ignominious death of Jesus. In their minds, their coming together after their fragmentation came about because they could not get Jesus out of their minds: they wanted to talk about him. And as they talked through their experience of him they found that, as they saw it, there was no explanation by reference to any of the language within their Jewish traditions. They were forced 'back' to Yahweh, to God himself, for an explanation. Yahweh was not, of course, 'outside' the Jewish tradition; Yahweh was the One who had called the Jews into being in the first place. But the consequence was that Christians, in order to be true to their experience, found themselves developing a language about God that while analogous with that of Judaism was different.

Both Christians and Jews knew God in their history. The

Jews knew God had rescued them from slavery in Egypt: Yahweh had brought them into the Promised Land. This, they came to see, could not have happened unless God was the Lord of creation as well as the Lord of history. Hence they understood God to be Creator, full of loving-kindness and truth; it was by his power that the Israelites had been redeemed from Egypt and called to declare God's promise to, presence with and loving-kindness for his whole world. The Christian community of faith was drawn to bring its experience of Jesus into relationship with Yahweh, and to see him as the fulfilment of Jewish prophecy and the embodiment of God's promise through it, to the whole creation. Jesus was the one through whom God declared indelibly his victory over death, hell and all evil. All people were in principle already saved: all people would, if they so chose, ultimately be saved.

John put it like this in his Gospel. Since Jesus was the intimate Word of God through whom everything was made, there was nothing outside the authority that God had given him. Jesus, the Word of God, said this with his life, so that the world could see for itself the ineradicable nature of God's living presence with his people. 'The light shines in the darkness, and the darkness did not overcome it,' says John.[10] And Paul declares, 'If God is for us, who is against us?'[11] He confidently goes on to claim God's complete triumph in history and creation over anything that challenges the fulfilment of his purpose in creating. 'For I am convinced that neither death, nor life, nor angels, nor rulers, nor things present, nor things to come, nor powers, nor height, nor depth, nor anything else in all creation, will be able to separate us from the love of God in Christ Jesus our Lord.'[12]

This mighty claim is all very well, but what does it amount to? The community of faith was set in a real world, not abstracted from it; there were questions to be addressed. The early Christians found them no easier to answer than we do. It is, of course, an everyday question as well as a theoretical matter: it is not enough to come up with ideas, useful though that is; the discovery of truth, as Jesus knew only too well, depends upon the experiment of living it out in life and, one must also add, in one's death. And don't let us forget that all these practical questions were arising in the turmoil of puzzled reflection, anxiety and excitement about the meaning of Jesus' life and death. The Easter greeting is profoundly moving. 'He is risen!' 'He is risen, indeed!' Isn't he?

One of the first questions for Christians was what to do about their relationship with the Jewish communities on which they depended. Their families may have continued to worship in the synagogue. Should they, could they? If Jesus was the fulfilment of Jewish prophecy, why should they not continue to worship there? But they were not welcome; they were seen to claim for Jesus an authority alien to Judaism, which indeed amounted to blasphemy. Jesus was God. Christians may not have known what exactly they meant by this claim, any more than we do if we have any sense. But certainly they wanted to hold together, as we do, language about Jesus and language about God. If Jesus was not to be confused with God – and that, Christians were clear they should not do – they wanted to claim that Jesus revealed God. Jesus had shown them what God was like, what human nature was about, and what God's purpose was in creating. Indeed it was more than that; the more they thought about it, they came to believe that Jesus did not simply show them God, he declared in himself the very nature and being of God's love, something that could not be separated from God himself. They must have found themselves tongue-tied in wanting to discuss it, explain it and encourage others to join them. And yet this was something else that they believed they were called to do. Not that they thought they had all the answers to everybody's questions; but they did think they had things to say that would encourage people to find God for themselves, and begin to follow 'in the way'. 'Let's walk together with Jesus and see whether in conversation with him we come to see God as clearly as he did?' But it meant they could no longer worship in the synagogue.

Well, if they were not able to associate with the synagogue, as many would undoubtedly have wanted to do, could they nevertheless be certain that if others came to join their community, they should first be introduced to the ways of Jewish worship? The matter was a live one. Gentiles had started to enquire about the faith, attracted by the dynamic preaching of Peter and Paul. What should be said to them? Peter was clear; Christians were Jews really, and should therefore be circumcised and be taught to refrain from eating forbidden foods. Paul, seeing that this would inhibit the preaching of the gospel to non-Jews, opposed him. He won. God was, as the Jews themselves understood really, God of the whole world and of all people, hence the good news that the community of faith found in Jesus was for all. It was not necessary to become a Jew first. This, Paul believed, did not bring into question the fundamental role that the Jewish people had played (and properly understood we should say *still play*, shouldn't we?) in God's salvation of the world.

These issues were just the tip of the iceberg: there was a lot of learning to do. The new community of faith was caught up in a world dominated by powers beyond its control. Most particularly, there was the power of Rome. Christians proclaimed Jesus to be Lord. For the Romans there was only one lord, and he was Caesar, the emperor for whom they also claimed divinity. Should they pay taxes to Caesar? The scribes posed the same question to Jesus, presenting him with a coin on which there was Caesar's superscription. Jesus' answer was perplexingly ambiguous, 'Give to the emperor what belongs to the emperor, and to God the things that are God's.'[13] Fine, but which exactly is which? But that is the point – we have to think about it: there are no simple answers. For Paul, it was a matter both of recognizing the role of the state in securing order, peace and justice, and also of giving God due worship; the two should be seen in association since no secular power would exist but for the fact that God permitted it.[14]

But even then, of course, there are many issues to consider. May not the state act unjustly? Suppose, as not infrequently was the case, the state persecuted Christians; what happened when Christians tried to subvert the state and impose theocratic government? The fact that the state is permitted by God to exercise power, but that it may act unjustly, means that careful attention may have to be given to the question of legitimate revolt. There might even arise the matter of assassination: Bonhoeffer thought so in respect of Hitler. There are, yet again, no final answers, no foolproof solutions. Dynamic conversation, careful examination of the facts, and above all the desire to know and find God, are irreducible aspects of faithful Christian living. They still are; thank God!

What about family life? When a person becomes a Christian, what does that mean for his or her family? A sharp question arises about divorce. According to Matthew, things were as they were in Judaism, in one respect at least. If a man wishes to divorce his wife he must officially give her a certificate of divorce. But there is more to it, for a man who divorces his wife makes her an adulteress, and anyone who marries a divorced woman commits adultery.[15] The only exception is when the married woman has herself committed adultery. But wait a minute, the meaning of this is far from clear. For one could argue that the assumption is precisely what one might expect – since one must assume that marriage makes a couple 'one flesh', in the event of a divorce the marriage cannot really have taken place. Therefore, however, if the 'marriage' had been consummated, there must necessarily have been adultery. But there's more to it; the argument within the community of faith must have been vivid and very personal.

Mark tells of an occasion when the Pharisees faced Jesus with the question, 'Is it lawful for a man to divorce his wife?' They, of course, were not interested in the actual answer to the question but with Jesus' attitude to the Mosaic law. Jesus sees through them and draws from them the legal position. But he goes on to suggest that it was only because they could not see the real point of marriage, that the two become one flesh, but regarded it as little more than a legal transaction, that Moses allowed the writing of certificate of divorcement. If they understood the intention behind marriage, they would see that there could be no such thing as divorce. 'Therefore what God has joined together, let no one separate.'[16]

The family is at its best a context of fruitful conversation. But one can imagine the issues that arose for the early

Christian community. Suppose a devout couple found their daughter anxious to marry a non-believer, what should they do? Should a Christian marry a non-believer? In the second letter to the Corinthians, Paul says in principle, 'No way!' He does not mince his words. 'Do not be mismatched with unbelievers. For what partnership is there between righteousness and lawlessness? Or what fellowship is there between light and darkness? What agreement does Christ have with Beliar? Or what does a believer share with an unbeliever? What agreement has the temple of God with idols?'[17] It's powerful and distressing stuff if one takes it at face value. Many of us may recall incidents when families have been destroyed by the blatant bigotry of certainties and the consequent unwillingness to learn. I remember one Methodist minister telling his daughter to leave home when he discovered that she intended to marry a Roman Catholic! Happily we have moved on from there. Surely love is the basis of a fine human relationship as it is of the relationship that, Christians believe, God has committed himself to in Christ. And God is committed to all, believer and unbeliever alike; he is committed to the whole world. But isn't it different if one of the couple becomes Christian after they have married, or if one member of a marriage ceases to be of the faith?

The questions are endless: slavery, usury, financial support for the apostles, preachers and teachers are just some that arise and are discussed in the New Testament. Should Christians be free to pursue any career of their choice? Should they fight for the emperor? Should they fight at all? Should they rather be pacifists? And never mind about paying taxes: we have seen some of the difficulties raised by that demand. However, given that Paul seems to have thought that the secular authority had legitimate authority, could a Christian be a tax-gatherer, a government official? They could apparently be tradesmen, carpenters, even shepherds. The Gospels associate shepherds with the birth of Christ and 'shepherd' was a title that Jesus associated with his own work. He used the image when calling Peter to follow him. 'Tend my sheep', he said. But shepherds were among the most despised members of Jewish society since the nature of their work, out all night and looking after filthy animals, meant that they were as likely as not to be ritually unclean. It was of no interest to Jesus apparently; they were all citizens of God's kingdom. Or could be.

Apparently new questions arise for us all the time. The New Testament does not discuss nuclear power, hedge funds, stem cell research, the internal combustion engine, the world wide web or air travel. What can we say about them? What counts is our willingness to come to terms with new situations and to learn from them. Abandonment of a problem in the face of a new difficulty, or refusal to deal with new ones, is out of the question if one's faith is grounded in the God of Jesus Christ: that is, the truth to which the New Testament bears witness. Nothing is or should be outside the interest and concern of Christians in the world where God has set them. Hoping to learn from experience, trying to discover the facts, and learning to test the spirits whether they be good or bad are tasks from which Christians cannot withdraw. In matters of public and private morality, the Church has rightly continued the quest for wisdom in human affairs.

One dimension of the situation in which the early Church found itself may well have added to the tension. How long had they got? I have laid emphasis on the fact that the Jewish tradition was based upon a future realization of God's promise to Abraham and Isaac and Jacob. Each time there seemed to be the potential for its immediate fulfilment, things went wrong. They were rescued from Egypt, but they were pursued by troubles even in the Promised Land, and only God's presence gave them the victory over their enemies. Then, when they might have hoped to settle down in a land flowing with milk and honey, with every man under his own palm tree, by a never-emptying oasis of still water with flocks and herds, and comforts galore sufficient to satisfy their every need – even then they were defeated and carried off into exile. They returned from exile and rebuilt the temple, but again things went badly and they were subject to devastation and conquest as well as moral turpitude from within their own society. But in the face of this they expected God to intervene directly, and to make his presence known before all the peoples. God would redeem his people; they were confident. The expectation flourished during the period that saw the rise of Christianity.

Given this tense background of anxiety and expectation, were Christians themselves to expect the imminent arrival of the kingdom? Is this what Jesus had expected? It is possible, as I have suggested, that the disciples themselves had misread the signs and believed that Jesus did expect the end in his lifetime or at the latest with his death. Perhaps they even tried to force the pace. But they were wrong.

Perhaps this meant that they were waiting for his return, but if so how could they read the signs and calculate the date of Jesus' return? Would it be right to look for martyrdom in order to be with Christ and all the angels in heaven? Or was it enough to accept martyrdom if it came their way? Was Jesus, as some scholars have suggested, actually a revolutionary leader who sought to build a kingdom of God on earth? Paul turned to the Gentiles and sought to bring them into the kingdom, but was he in fact trying to build up a righteous army of moral soldiers against the persecution of the Roman empire? Had he visions of fulfilling Christ's purpose in the world by attacking the forces of evil as presented by totalitarian powers, unjust systems and all the powers of evil? Was he fighting to free humanity from thrall to illusion and evil? All these questions were, and sadly still are, currently in the minds of some groups within and without the Church. But if we are looking for a swift end, a final solution, and blinding revelation, we are mistaken. There are no such things for Christians or anyone else. What there is, is the puzzling, rewarding, demanding intriguing person of Jesus, whom we call the Christ. Who is he?

It took some time for the community of faith to sort these things out, and to create a perspective on things that was commensurate with their growing understanding of the power and grace of God as revealed in Christ. It was very hard work. Any reading of the New Testament will confirm this. It is important to read whole books, of course, and not just your own or another person's favourite verses. One has to make one's own way, listen to what others have said, look at some useful commentaries, take advice on what books are worth reading that will illuminate the period, and get stuck into the conversation.

The conversation that God began with his world in creating, which he continued in the calling of the Israelites, is the same conversation into which Jesus introduced his disciples. We continue it today, fitfully and sometimes unbelievingly. It came to formal expression in the decisions of the institutional Church that emerged over the centuries via ecumenical councils and its organization under local 'overseers' whom we call bishops, whose authority was established under the Servant of the servants of God, the Bishop of Rome, the Pope. Whatever the ecclesial structure, whether it be Anglican, Lutheran, Reformed, Baptist or Methodist, or whatever, it has to define its position in relation to this central and continuing tradition; if it does not, it brings into question whether its conversation, which may of course be *about* Jesus and God, is indeed *coherent with* the conversation of the community of faith with God in Christ.

Sadly, the Church has from time to time itself frustrated the conversation by attempting to define what is to be believed, and therefore what is to be taught, instead of relying upon the good faith of members of the community to engage in conversation and to report their experience. There is, of course, a role for central authority; somewhere there must be a guardian of the tradition, but it should be based upon encouraging the business of the tradition in learning to hope, not about defining the words of what to teach and how to teach it. Learning is all of a piece. I have come across many a would-be mathematician who has been very good at remembering a proof, but who has no understanding of what it is about; many a would-be historian who can recite the dates of the kings and queens of England, who has no insight into the nature of history. There have been too many authorities in the Church, theological and ecclesial, whose concern has been to live by the law, rather than the Spirit. Wanting God is what we have to learn to do if we are to be participant in the conversation of the faithful with God in Christ.

The community of faith is called to extend the conversation of God with his world to include people of all faiths and none, all dimensions of knowledge developed in whatever discipline of enquiry, and all insights offered in the arts of all kinds, so that the unity of God's creation and the one human community of faith can be freely enjoyed by all. It isn't easy, but that's the task. And as we understand it, we cannot ultimately fail, because the world is God's, if only we had the mind of Christ to see it and the love of Christ actually to want it.

5

It Isn't Easy, Is It?

No, it certainly isn't! But that does not mean that it is dull, or that it shouldn't be enjoyable. The Church has found it hard at every stage of its history. There have been good times for sure, but all too frequently there have been the bad times to endure when things just didn't seem to make sense. The same is true for the average Christian in everyday life; it only sometimes makes sense. Even belief in the fundamentals of the faith can be transient as we move from one crisis to another and have to set about once again trying to put things and our selves together. Often the best we can do is to take seriously Cleo Laine's demanding encouragement, 'The Least You Can Do Is the Best You Can'.[1]

When trying to take account of the fact that the Christian life is difficult, it is well to remind ourselves of a couple of things. First, the life of faith wasn't easy for the Israelites. They had a marvellous promise of salvation, as they understood it – a divine promise. There was to be a land flowing with milk and honey, there was release from slavery. There were indeed, make no mistake about it, huge successes; but failure and disappointment stared them in the face at almost every step. They were nevertheless called to be faithful and to believe that they were under the protection of Yahweh.

For the most part it was hard work, though from time to time there were dramatic signs. Take, for example, the capture of Jericho. They were a nomadic people who had pursued their enemies to the powerful walled city of Jericho. They were stuck. What possible chance had they to take it? Yet their attack was successful. Joshua, under instruction from the Lord, had told them what to do.[2] They were to march around the city once on each of six successive days with seven priests blowing their trumpets before the ark of the Lord. On the seventh day the seven priests with seven trumpets were to lead them round the city seven times, and when the priests blew the trumpets all the people were to shout 'with a great shout' and charge the walls. They followed the Lord's commands to the letter and when the trumpets blew the walls fell down flat. Fantastic!

But surely common sense tells us – and must have told them – that it was all normal and entirely explicable in simple military and psychological terms. Perhaps all that had happened was that they performed a ritual act in which by circling a space they dedicated everything within it to God. The destruction that followed the victory would indicate that this is a possibility. Encouraged by this performance, when the trumpet actually sounded they attacked Jericho with all the might they could muster. The call of the trumpet by the priests was a sign not only that they should commence their attack but also that God had already given them the victory. As Paul might have said in similar circumstances, 'If God is with us, who can be against us?' But it didn't matter to them how it happened, it was the Lord's doing really. How else would a pathetic nomadic tribe capture a strongly defended large walled city? The Israelites could only make sense of their victory by bringing Yahweh into the conversation; at least the person or persons behind the book of Joshua, possibly written in the seventh century BC, thought so.

More characteristically, however, the history of Judaism was one of sadness and despair in which it was necessary to work very hard to retain faith in God's promise. How can this have come about since God, Yahweh, was the only real power and his promise was to be trusted? The nation and individual believers were puzzled. The book of Job explores the possibility that his disasters are his own fault; they must be – his 'friends' are quite clear about this. Lamentations offers some modest hope for the exiles, but ends attempting to face up to the possibility that God might have rejected them for ever. 'Restore us to yourself, O Lord, that we may be restored; renew our days as of old – unless you have utterly rejected us, and are angry with us beyond measure?'[3]

Many of the Psalms, which formed part of their community worship, express the poignant anxiety of a suffering people in disturbing language. God cannot be blamed, their disasters must be their fault; their failures in faithful living lead inevitably to their discomfort.

Psalm 130
Out of the depths I cry to you, O LORD.
Lord, hear my voice!
Let your ears be attentive
to the voice of my supplications!

If you, O LORD, should mark iniquities,
Lord, who could stand?
But there is forgiveness with you,
so that you may be revered.

I wait for the LORD, my soul waits, and in his word I hope;
my soul waits for the Lord
more than those who watch for the morning,
more than those who watch for the morning.

O Israel, hope in the LORD!
For with the LORD there is steadfast love,
and with him is great power to redeem.
It is he who will redeem Israel
from all its iniquities.

The prophets are ambiguous; yes, it is their own fault, they have neglected to be faithful, but there is hope. Even Jeremiah, often thought of as the prophet of doom, has hope in God. And properly understood, the prophetic vision is based not on future prediction, but on a right reading of how things really are now, if only they took God and his promises seriously. In the period of the Babylonian exile (589–537 BC) there was a more luminous vision to put alongside the dismal one provided in the book of Lamentations: this was the work of a prophet whom we know as Deutero-Isaiah, the writer or editor of chapters 40—55 of the present book. He associates their suffering with their witness to the fulfilment of God's promise. Truth and justice, peace and wisdom are hard-won properties; they flow from the willing determination to see things through in the light of faith. The writer personalizes it in the Suffering Servant Songs, those magical verses that constitute some of the most inspirational poetry in the Old Testament.[4] The Suffering Servant has been variously interpreted as the righteous remnant of Israel, an individual kingly inheritor of the house of David, a mythological hero, or, more unlikely but just possible, a pre-figuring of the messiah anticipating the birth of Jesus. The most important feature of the prophecy is the association of the process of the fulfilment of Israel's hope with suffering, unsought but accepted on behalf of all and potentially revelatory of the kingdom. Far from being the sign of the end of their hope, their suffering was the unimaginable beginning of its realization.

Second, Jesus himself did not find it easy to make sense of his faith in God, if indeed he ever did in this lifetime. He seems to have believed that it was possible to do so, and that was enough for him. It was not all plain sailing, however. That there could be suffering associated with the ministry to which he felt himself called, Jesus seems to have understood from the beginning. In thinking through their life with Jesus afterwards, the writers of the Gospels seem to have felt this to be the case, though there is plenty of evidence that they resisted the idea whenever they came across it. They didn't want to be part of a suffering kingdom but a victorious kingdom! Mark reports that James and John, the sons of Zebedee, come to Jesus and request to sit on the left and right side of Jesus in his glory. He properly points out that they have no idea what they are talking about, unless they are willing to share his cup of suffering![5]

To my mind, the continuous misunderstanding that Jesus faced must have been a severe test to him and even led him from time to time to question himself and his mission. Whenever it seemed that he was making progress, the contrary turned out to be the case. He healed a man with a withered arm, so Mark reports, but all the Pharisees were interested in was his attitude to the rules of the sabbath.[6] (By the way, not everything is as it seems in the Gospels. For example, the writers unjustly treat the Pharisees – total vilification is mistaken, or so many scholars now believe.) When his disciples began to pluck ears of corn, again according to Mark, the Pharisees were only concerned to point out Jesus' disregard for the law.[7] The law was clear, nothing should be done on the sabbath: absolutely no work at all! But what counted as work? There was a whole tradition of legal interpretation of the matter so that the merest issue could be settled by reference to its clear teaching. But for Jesus it all seems to miss the point. Jesus' exasperation is clear from the words Mark puts into his mouth. 'The sabbath was made for humankind, not humankind for the sabbath; so the Son of Man is lord even of the sabbath.'[8] God didn't create a space for nothing, call it the sabbath, and then create man so that there was someone who could do nothing on the sabbath!

The apparent impossibility of bringing those with whom he associated into conversation with the God of Abraham, Isaac and Jacob can only have depressed him. Nobody seemed to get the point, whether it was his immediate disciples, a wider community of interested followers, or the day-by-day groups with whom he naturally came into contact as he went about his business of trying to talk the language of God with them, in the marketplace, the countryside and the synagogue. All this makes the words of Jesus in response to the thief who shared his ignominious death on the cross utterly remarkable. The criminal says, or so Luke has it, 'Jesus, remember me when you come into your kingdom.' Jesus replies, 'Truly, I tell you, today you will be with me in Paradise.'[9] If nothing else, this would suggest that however difficult it is to remain faithful to the business of learning to hope, it is possible. Does the eschaton, 'the beginning of the next things', happen with this exchange? It's an interesting thought.

The questions pile up for the Church. Some are utterly fundamental. If God is perfectly good, all-knowing, all-loving and absolutely powerful, why doesn't he do something about the evil and suffering so apparent in the world?

Discussion on this central matter is as old as history and not confined to Christianity. Yet there are for the Christian useful, significant ways of getting involved in a conversation about it. Let's begin with God, as Christians understand him. If God wants to share his own nature of love with a world that is other than him, then he will have to allow it a freedom analogous to the freedom God would have to enjoy in choosing to create it; God would have to want to do so freely. Otherwise what sense can we make of God as loving? Love that is not freely given is hardly love! Even in human relationships, one of the conditions of accepting that someone loves us is that their love is freely given, and not the product of cash, power or undue influence. This is exactly what Christians believe God set out to do in creating; to make a world that could enjoy for itself and for its own sake the sort of love God enjoyed in himself.

When Christians talk of God freely choosing to create, they also implicitly accept, at any rate in theory, that God was willing to take the risk of failure. What would happen if the world took its life into its own hands and chose unwisely to ignore its own nature, or to try to live in denial of it? What would God do then? But failure would be an unreasonable outcome for God, since his nature would be the same before and after this possible outcome. So if he was to proceed in accordance with the desire within him and go on to create, he would have to be willing to pay the price, accept the cost. Which is precisely what the Christian community says that God did, *and does*! In technical theological language, we say that God creates by his grace, but also acknowledge, as Bonhoeffer rightly said, 'there is no such thing as cheap grace'.[10] So God took the cost on himself; there was no other Being who could do so – there *is* no other being! Hence the language of God's loving and the language of Jesus' sacrifice are bound together in the single theological language of the Christian faith. God in creating committed himself to making a success of what he had begun. I suggest that teachers and parents have an inkling of what is going on here. When once one is committed to a child it is to a particular child and not just to children in the abstract. One had better remember, therefore, if one is to enjoy it and make a success of it, that whatever the circumstances in which the child finds herself, it will not be money or time or information or simple care that is required, it is the gift of oneself. What one begins in love, one will want to see through to the end whatever the cost. Such is the nature of love.

Of course, something of the same kind might be said of every other important relationship that is involved in the flourishing of the human condition or, as one might say, the fulfilment of God's purpose in creating. For the more one thinks of what is demanded of one as a parent in contributing to the successful living of a life by another independent human being, the more one realizes that one cannot do it on one's own; the willing and affectionate concern of the child for his or her own well-being has to be won. And it is a costly process, but this is where we began. As we are required to work in affectionate partnership with a person who is independent of us if we are to achieve our purpose, so also is God in his creative purpose. The commitment to create implies a continuing commitment to recreate in the face of difficulty, perplexity and fear; in the case of God we call it redemptive creativity. God will never give up and abandon the world to its own devices; it would be contrary to his nature to do so. He gladly bears the pain to the end.

It is hard though to believe it. Death, pain, injustice, cruelty, misrepresentation, despair, failure, mistaken choices, deliberate evil behaviour – all undermine any sense that the world is the work of an all-loving, omnipotent, omniscient Creator, who is committed now and always to making a success of what he has set himself to do. There's too much evidence to the contrary, surely. As Anthony Flew once wrote of the Christian position as a whole in famous contributions to a discussion in *University*, the Christian theologian's claim that God is both all-loving and omnipotent is meaningless and 'dies the death of a thousand qualifications' in the face of ordinary human experience'.[11] And he rejects the so-called Freewill Defence in an intriguing if somewhat far-fetched argument in which he tries to show that human freedom and divine foreknowledge are compatible really, so whereas God could have created a world in which everyone would want to do his will, he chose not to.[12] Clearly there is work to be done, if we are to make any sense of the world we find ourselves in and hold it together with a living faith in God as the Christian community conceives him to be.

The work necessary to getting to grips with this and the many other questions concerning faith has to be engaged in actively; one has to want to do it. Like any learning, it has to be done by the individual concerned; it cannot be done for them. But there will have to be a framework of signs to which one is introduced, if one is to have the tools to begin the job. Most fundamentally, one needs to be introduced to the language if one is to talk the talk and live the Christian life. No physicist will understand physics if he or she lacks the language of physics; he or she will not be able to devise an experiment, know how to carry one out or learn from its results. Hence there is analogously a framework of word and action in which Christians can begin to find their way around and share in the conversation from their personal points of view.

The framework is provided by worship, sacramental word and action, and conversation in family, school and the wider society of the Church. Learning to participate in it will enable one to attend to one's own questions, improve one's capacity to contribute to the conversation and build a personal interior life. Above all, perhaps, it offers a river of experience and wisdom into which, at times of pressure and confusion, one can dip, remind oneself of where one began and begin all over again the conversation of faith from a new perspective. I shall focus on the two sacraments of Baptism, and the Eucharist or Mass (also variously called Holy Communion, The Lord's Supper, depending upon the Christian tradition). I shall deal first with Baptism.

Christian initiation is a most important matter. When in doubt about his standing in the faith, Martin Luther reminded himself, '*Baptizatus sum*' – 'I have been baptized!' That seems to have renewed his sense of being a real self by affirming his place in God's presence. Human beings have always sought certainties. Descartes is often regarded as the first modern philosopher; he wanted to identify something of which he could be certain in a world he experienced to be subject to decay and where nothing seemed ultimately to be reliable. What experience was indubitable? *'Cogito ergo sum'* – 'I think, therefore I am'; that was where he believed he could begin if he was to build up secure knowledge of the world. Since I am thinking, I must exist! What he thought he could build on this included, remarkably and in fact unbelievably, the existence of God!

For Luther, security and hope were grounded in the fact of his baptism: 'I have been baptized'. Perhaps for the Christian it is better to say, *'Dubito ergo sum'* – 'I doubt, therefore I am'; in my view as Christians we must first acknowledge our human doubt before we can reasonably begin to understand what we believe. It is precisely this freedom to doubt that is implied in the freedom of God's gracious creating, for it, in turn, guarantees the continuous opportunity to question and therefore to grow in understanding. On this depends any possibility there may be that we shall learn to hope. I shall return to this below, in Chapter 9.

But what does baptism mean? Its importance is obvious since it has been part of the tradition from the very beginning, as references to it in the Acts and the Pauline epistles testify. Indeed, we know that John, the precursor of Jesus, according to the tradition was known as 'the Baptizer', so the idea of ritual purification in some form was familiar in Judaism. But it had a new meaning for Christians who, tradition has it, were commanded by the risen Christ to baptize all nations. The Great Commission, as it is called, is very powerful stuff. Jesus came and said to them, 'All authority in heaven and on earth has been given to me. Go therefore and make disciples of all nations, baptizing them in the name of the Father and of the Son and of the Holy Spirit, and teaching them to obey everything that I have commanded you. And remember, I am with you always, to the end of the age.'[13]

Jesus had, through his baptism by John the Baptist, taken upon himself the representative role of humankind in the presence of the Father, a role that was fulfilled in his death, resurrection *and* ascension. Thus when Paul talks of baptism as incorporation into Christ, he means that since this representative man included all persons in his dying and rising, all persons baptized into him can share in the same victory of good over evil, truth over falsity, justice over injustice, life over death. Jesus' commission to the disciples is that they are to introduce everyone, all nations, into the liberty of his conversation with God. The community of faith, of which each baptized person is a member, has, potentially, a part to play in furthering God's creative purpose. The baptismal liturgy presents this good news. The reading of the Gospel declares it, parents acknowledge that this is what they believe and what they want for their child; they are supported by godparents and by the local community representing the universal Church, for no one can undertake such responsibilities on their own. Language is public, not private, as Wittgenstein pointed out. In the early Church baptism took place symbolically, after careful preparation, at either Easter or Pentecost in order to underline their relationship with the life of Jesus and the birth of the Church.

Most churches acknowledge that baptism is a once-and-for-all event. Hence Luther's confidence! Once baptized, always baptized; incorporation into Christ is an indelible matter. There have, therefore, from time to time been legalistic and mechanical approaches to baptism suggesting that once one was baptized one could do whatever one liked and still rely on salvation because one was incorporated into the risen Christ. Hence there have been those who have taken the safety-net route and believed that the death-bed is the place and time for baptism! Such legalistic interpretations are no better than the legalistic approaches to the sabbath.

Baptism is only a beginning; one has to make one's own contribution to the conversation into which one has been introduced and make it one's own. The conversation may have begun, but it has to continue. We know now just how early a child's understanding and linguistic skills are stimulated into activity by being present during family conversations and how dependent a child is on the linguistic world in which he or she is set. The development of Christian faith depends upon the same realization. At some stage – it varies in the many Christian traditions – confirmation is the occasion when a person is confirmed in their faith: it is as if it is now acknowledged that a person has begun to take responsibility for his or her own learning, always remembering that at no stage in life can one rely exclusively on one's own capacities.

Even when set in the framework of faith by baptism and encouraged to take up one's own part in the community of faith by confirmation, there is nobody who will find it easy to believe. The major reason for this is that the greater one's hopes, the more likely they are to be dashed by experience. And what we are introduced to in baptism is the conversation of Jesus with God the Father, in which it is asserted that the creation is good because it is the work of God who has committed himself to it and will never abandon it to its own devices. It is a world, therefore, in which we can work with confidence for human flourishing in the best and broadest sense. This is an exciting vision, which is all too often obscured by war, human cruelty and natural disaster. Added to which the baptized person will from time to time find herself in a society where such faith is ridiculed, the truth mocked, and where faithful believing is counter-cultural.

Many regard the present period of history in Western Europe to be just such a time. What count as success are fulfilment of ambition in trivial matters, winning the lottery, having a good time, possessing glamour, money, power and influence, being young and attractive. They should never be ridiculed; these are aspects of life that when regarded as gifts of God in a good world can be thoroughly enjoyed, used well and, in the best sense, profitably. It is after all the *worship* of money that is the root of evil, not its possession. But it is often said now, more fundamentally and more damagingly, that there are no ultimate truths, only bits and pieces of knowledge which, if one is in the right place at the right time, one can deploy persuasively in order to get one's own way. It is frequently put in this form and called postmodernism; there are no longer believable meta-narratives with which to tell life's story and hold together the whole of life's meaning.

But this is just what the Christian tradition wants to claim. We believe that there is a universal narrative, the speaking of which will introduce one to clues with which to make sense of life. To go on trying to tell such a story and continue the process of learning to hope, one needs encouragement.

The Eucharist provides the continuous underpinning of the framework of Christian living. Regular participation in its celebration reminds one of the grounds of one's faith, feeds one with the truth of Christ, and commissions the believer again for the work of God in the world. It confirms the promise of Jesus: 'And remember, I am with you always, to the end of the age.' There is a Jewish background to this sacrament. The Passover meal recalls the Exodus, and in particular the sprinkling of the blood of a slaughtered lamb over the lintel so that the Lord would 'pass over' the Israelites' houses when the first-born of Egypt were killed. The continuity of the conversation between the generations may be further attested to in that the meal may be the development of a tradition among nomadic people of the slaying of the firstborn. The story of the Exodus is recalled at each Passover in response to the enquiry of the youngest child, 'How is this night different from all other nights?'

Jesus invited his disciples to share in a meal on the evening before his arrest and crucifixion, though scholars debate whether or not it was an actual Passover meal. Certainly the supper was at the time of the Passover and closely associated with it in Christian tradition. At the meal, according to the Marcan tradition, Jesus takes bread, blesses it, breaks it and shares it with his disciples with the remarkable words, 'Take; this is my body.' He followed this by taking the cup of wine, usually shared among those present, gave thanks and gave it to them with the equally astonishing words, 'This is my blood of the covenant, which is poured out for many. Truly I tell you, I will never again drink of the fruit of the vine until that day when I drink it new in the kingdom of God.'[14] Paul, it is thought, preserves the earliest account of it, in which Jesus urges his disciples to do it as often as they do it, in remembrance of him.[15] Every occasion in which Christians celebrate the Eucharist they are to think of themselves as sharing in this meal with Christ. They should even entertain the imaginative perspective that in doing so they share in Jesus' cup of suffering, and therefore both now and prospectively in his glorious resurrection. Working out what that means takes a lifetime.

The meaning is, of course, contested. Is it a simple memorial? In which case do Christians do no more – and no less! – than recall thankfully what happened two millennia ago? Jesus was crucified, and in so doing gave his life for the salvation of humankind. The theological background to such thinking requires some careful examination. Did God require such a sacrifice *before* he could fulfil his purpose in creating? Is the fact that the world had turned in on itself and done what was good in its own eyes such a heinous matter that there was no good thing left in the world? If so, where does the claim of both Jews and Christians stand, that God saw the world he was creating, and 'behold it was very good!'

In the light of such a claim surely Rahner's emphasis is significant: 'there is no such thing as ungraced nature'; or therefore I would add to make it explicit, 'no such thing as ungraced human nature'. But since I hold this to be true, the community of faith is doing more in the Eucharist than merely remembering what has happened. This is not like remembering Dunkirk, or the day one inherited the family estate. The community of faith, in word and action, actually takes part in the making and remaking of the world, with God in Christ, through the Holy Spirit. We remember not the past, but remind ourselves of what is actually going on now and our part in it – if only we had eyes to see it. God is indeed redemptively creating the world and using us in this work, as he must; it is true. By sharing in the Passion of Christ, we share in his resurrection and therefore in the work of creating to which God is committed. If we take seriously what we are doing and saying in company with the whole Church, we are reminded (somewhat paradoxically) that we can both begin to take part in the conversation with God to which Jesus has introduced us all over again, *and* develop further whatever understanding we already have.

It is hardly to be wondered at that the conversation is not

yet completely intelligible – as Paul pointed out, we only know in part.[16] The separation of God and the world seems so obvious to us in everyday life, that we have from time to time set about accustoming ourselves to its consequences: we've tried to do the best we can in the circumstances. But what we have sometimes feared to be the case is simply false. The human and the divine are not divided, but are one in Christ without diminishment of the reality of either the divine or the human. Theologians took centuries to work out a way of saying that it was worth thinking about; there were many debates and controversies, but they are now summed up in claiming for Jesus humanity and divinity, without confusion of natures or wills. The life that God promised his world in creating it is possible; we know this because what he has begun we can see he has committed himself in Christ to making a success of. The community of faith can bear witness to the truth of God's promise because it has been fulfilled in Christ. Jesus has enacted in himself that partnership of the divine and the human in his own birth, life and teaching, death, resurrection and ascension. What began with God will end in God. In Jesus, whom we called the Christ, there is demonstrated what we are always inclined to doubt: the real presence of God with his world and his people. Reminding ourselves of this fact in eucharistic celebration sets us off again, renewed in the truth that 'faith, hope, and love abide, these three; and the greatest of these is love'.[17]

It is important to mark the beginning in which, of course, all later development is implicit – 'in my beginning is my end' – so that anyone may baptize; it certainly used, for example, to be part of the training of every nurse in the United Kingdom. In the event of an emergency a nurse would make the sign of the cross with water on the patient's forehead (usually a baby's), and baptize in the name of the Father, and of the Son and of the Holy Spirit. All traditions tend to accept that this is proper and pastorally important. The circumstance is different in the case of the Eucharist, where the *essential* nature of the celebration is such that the person who presides and represents the one and only celebrant, Christ, has traditionally if not invariably been an ordained minister. The liturgy must be conducted with order and decorum; there must be the possibility of discipline if the service is done frivolously without due sense of the fact of God's mysterious, forgiving and life-giving presence with his people. Paul had occasion to call congregations to remember their responsibilities in his time; the Church has a continuing duty to do so to this day. Hence the continuation of the tradition that it is a dimension of the work of the ordained person, the priest, to celebrate such a basic reminder of the real nature of things in God's world. In some Protestant traditions this is questioned; Methodism authorizes lay people to celebrate in some circumstances, and even the Anglican Communion is threatened with controversy about lay celebration in one or two provinces, such as Australia where the Bishop of Sydney is promoting the cause of lay administration. For the most part, however, the tradition remains; celebration of the sacraments is what ordination includes – at least.

If baptism concerns the introduction to the conversation with God to which Jesus introduced us, and the Eucharist the regular reminder that it is possible to enjoy it and share in the creation and recreation of God's world, we are also reminded that the Church has taught that death is a dimension of that recreation. Learning to hope is not limited to this world; learning to hope involves opening up the question of whether the term 'life after death' has any meaning. I believe that it does. Most particularly it has a meaning within the communion of saints. All persons who have wanted to love God, want to love God now and who will in future generations want to love God are included with this communion. There is no division in the communion of saints between the living and the dead, and the yet to be born, since all are one in Christ. Hence it is reasonable to think that one can stand within that communion and, in the presence of Christ, pray for the dead, those who are alive now, and for future generations. If, as we believe, the central sacrament of Christian living is the Church itself, the thought that the dead are not alive in Christ is intolerable. This does not mean, of course, that it is true. It does mean, however, that if Christians are not on the right lines in what they celebrate about God and God's relationship with the world in Christ, and that what they believe about God is untrue, they are of all people most miserable. One's mind must be open to that possibility.

Hence the vital importance of bringing one's thinking about God and his nature as revealed in the person of Christ into relationship with one's own personal enquiring. In pursuit of this task, Charles Wesley's marvellous eucharistic hymns sometimes strike a chord that no others do.

Author of life divine,
Who hast a table spread,
Furnished with mystic wine
And everlasting bread,
Preserve the life thyself hast given,
And feed and train us up for heaven.

Our needy souls sustain
With fresh supplies of love,
Till all thy life we gain,
And all thy fullness prove,
And, strengthened by thy perfect grace,
Behold without a veil thy face.[18]

This conversation never ceases: we can always learn to hope.

6

Conversation with God:
Praying and Wanting

I remember being told in my confirmation class at St John's Methodist Church, Bangor (which consisted only of a couple of us!), that we should follow Jesus' example and pray regularly. When, some time later, I looked into the matter I found that we have no idea how frequently Jesus prayed. There is evidence that on occasions he attended the synagogue. We know also that he sought his own society sometimes. John, for example, refers to his withdrawing by himself after the feeding of the five thousand.[1] But should we literally understand by this that Jesus was 'on his own'? I suggest not. The fact is, it seems to me, that in the face of public misunderstanding and ignorance, Jesus sought to give his attention to God, his Father, in whose presence he believed himself to have his identity and to be himself. It was the nourishment he gained from faith in the Father that gave Jesus the strength to be the person he was. Hence the terrible significance in the awful, but in the event inspiring, words that, according to Mark he spoke from the cross in the presence of death: 'My God, my God, why have you forsaken me?'[2] In the face of the momentous gathering of hatred and mock triumph around him, Jesus' words express his fear of personal extinction: if God was not with him, there could be nothing to hope for. The use of the word 'my' is wounding: '*My* God'! Could any words of his utter more fully the agony of personal desolation!

But let's return to ponder Jesus' words in the Garden of Gethsemane and on the cross. Here there are, apparently but not really paradoxically, signs that the world is full of hope.

Jesus, according to Mark, symbolically moves away from his disciples and prays, 'Abba, Father, for you all things are possible; remove this cup from me; yet, not what I want, but what you want.'[3] This is not a simple statement that God knows best; it is a personal surrendering of his self to God in whose presence he believes. So when reflecting theologically on his experience of Jesus' preparation for the cross, John says that Jesus saw it all as manifesting God's glory, which we know in John's theology means the very presence of God himself. The world's life, and human life too, therefore – even including the Person of Jesus who himself shared with us the frailty of human life – depend upon God's awareness of us, not our awareness of God. The resurrection affirms this. As the tradition rightly has it, God raised Jesus from the dead; Jesus did not raise himself, nor was his resurrection a natural consequence of 'the good life' that he lived. So what Jesus confirms by his death on the cross, and what God affirms in the resurrection, is the eternal possibility of knowing and enjoying God, because the opportunity is bound in with the very nature of God himself, present, all-knowing, all-powerful and all-loving.

I recognize that it is not easy to live life on this basis because so much experience is against it – apparently. Hence it is important that baptized Christians meet regularly together in eucharistic celebration, in thankful reminder of God's nature and his very presence and in remembrance of what he has done in Christ. We need to be clear too that at each and every Eucharist God meets with the whole company of the faithful, which includes all who have died, are alive, and will live in the faith. Moreover, therefore, however small the actual gathering in a particular place, those few persons who are present incorporate the whole community of faith and offer to God in Christ the whole of creation, because God's presence is in the whole creation, not simply in the Church. The Church is not a body of people who are saved and so in some way taken out of the world to a safe haven; it is the Body of Christ which on behalf of the whole world bears witness to the true nature of God and therefore also to the true nature of God's creation.

This magnificent vision emboldens Christians in their believing and helps them to identify themselves with Christ's offering of himself on behalf of the world, and in so doing to begin dimly to understand Jesus' pain, and share in Christ's suffering. Christians too are likely to be misunderstood, and from time to time find life tough. Indeed, it is not simply that the world does not understand or want to know, Christians too, sadly, misunderstand and mistrust one another. Frustration can lead some to want to impose their will on the world or to confuse self-concern with an exercise of proper authority – if only the world would do what is perfectly obviously the right thing to do! We have to learn to resist such temptations. A realization that we must do this may lead us, as it did Jesus, to withdraw by ourselves. We do so in order to remember two things. First, we are not alone but in the presence of God, and second, the world in which we are set is God's creation, and good. Such praying is rooted in knowledge of our baptism into the Body of Christ, and the regular meeting of all Christian people in thankful celebration of the benefits of Christ's passion and the presence of the Holy Spirit.

So what of private prayer? Where does that fit in? The first thing to say is that since all prayer is in community, we will do well to talk of *personal* rather than private prayer. We think of ourselves as persons when we find ourselves affirmed by others in relationship. We become persons as we grow in our family, in school, in community, at work, among our peers, as we accept our responsibilities and duties, and find others acknowledging their responsibilities and duties towards us. In the case of our confession of Christian faith we acknowledge responsibilities and duties as members of the Church, as persons 'incorporated into the Body of Christ'. To be a Christian is to be in relationship with God through Christ, through whom we have our personal identity, and our *Christian* name. Personal prayer involves the appropriation into our own person of the public language of faith in word and sacrament, and living the gospel in our own lives. We pray in the prayer of humble access, 'Grant us therefore, Gracious Lord, so to eat the flesh of your dear Son Jesus Christ and to drink his blood, that our sinful bodies may be made clean by his body and our souls washed through by his most precious blood, and that we may evermore dwell in him, and he in us.' If we are to mean what we say in so praying, we have to affirm at all times in our saying and doing our awareness of God's presence with us and of our presence with him.

The intimacy of worship and belief, of praying and believing, is underlined in this style of life. As we believe, so we will pray. Our prayers reveal our theology. It was David Head who wrote scintillating prayers for all occasions.[4] One I recall concerned a mother arriving just in time for the morning service. 'O Lord, I did turn the gas down before I came out, didn't I! Amen.' Or have you heard of the undergraduate preparing for his examination in New Testament Greek, marvellously penitent and honest in his whole approach. 'I confess that I have done no work and cannot understand Greek, but as it is your will, O Lord, that I should pass my examinations, please tell me what to write when I face my examination tomorrow. Amen.' Or how do you react to the splendid inattention to the real world implicit in the Prayer of the Spiritual Cook's Tour? 'O God our Father, we pray for everyone in need: for the people of Outer Mongolia, the Seychelles and Gibraltar; for Iran, Iceland and Patagonia, for the lonely people of Tierra del Fuego and Alderney. And lastly, O Lord, we pray for those who have nobody to pray for them, those who live on uninhabited islands. Amen.' We need some common sense, some knowledge of the tradition, some knowledge of the world, some knowledge of ourselves and some knowledge of God, if we are to pray illuminatingly and hopefully. Praying and believing are one; bringing them together is a theological task.

Personal prayer begins and ends in praise and thanksgiving, as Neville Ward reminds us.[5] What other attitude could we have as persons in the presence of the Father! Even the most banal of sentiments can remind us of the truth. Take Claudius' harvest hymn, *Wir pflügen*, for example. The chorus runs:

All good gifts around us
   Are sent from heaven above;
Then thank the Lord, O thank the Lord,
   For all his love.

We may cringe at the words, even though the tune calls for lusty singing; they are so simplistic, uncontemporary and unsophisticated! But on reflection, the words say just what we feel and really want to sing at the top of our voices – in sheer, wholesome, delighted and renewing gratitude for God and his creation! And if it hurts because it also reminds us that our prayer is built into a belief that the *us* means *all of us*, and that among the *us* there is a sizeable minority (is it a third or a quarter of the world's population?), who do not enjoy the benefit of all God's good gifts, so much the better.

Indeed, if only we would learn to practise what we say we believe, then the live sense of gratitude that comes from knowing that the world is God's good gift to his people, and that he is present to bring it to perfection, might encourage us in our commitment to finding God's will and making the world a better place – for everyone. Such thankfulness is the ground of hope itself, for given the nature of God hope is not a future possibility, but a present reality – what we may be has already begun to be revealed – and enjoyed! – if we've got any sense. Christians are working with the grain of the universe.

We may know this and accept in theory its truth, but this does not necessarily mean that we practise what we preach, so confession is a proper response to our circumstances. Confession is not the result of guilt, for feelings of guilt are almost always paralysing. We confess because our thankfulness leads us to confess our faith and recall God to mind, in whom we live and move and have our being. God is not frightened away by our failures; indeed, our failures follow from our forgetfulness of him and a consequent assumption that we have to act on our own, within our own strength. We haven't, we can't. Bringing God to mind again, recognizing that he has been present the whole time, and that we can therefore *both* continue the conversation *and* begin it all over again is of the essence of every real relationship, most especially our relationship with God. Since he wills the good of all his creatures, we have nothing to fear.

If we are lucky, we will come across just such attitudes from time to time in our relationships with other people. The headmaster of Kingswood School when I was a pupil was A. B. Sackett. To be sent to him to read an essay, let alone for some misdemeanour, could be the occasion of anxiety. Down the passageway one went, towards the dining hall, turn right through the door into the corridor of his house, and then immediately left towards his study. In front at the end of the corridor covering the whole wall was a large mirror, so one watched oneself approach the door of the study, knock and enter. Actually, once inside and greeted by his infectious smile one felt strangely at home. One simply knew that whatever the outcome, his attention was on you and your well-being. One might even say if it was not so politically incorrect to say such things nowadays, that one knew that he loved you. On the total world scale, that is what Christians believe about God and our presence with him: God loves us. Whatever the situation, his attention is entirely focused on our personal well-being.

The confidence that flows from being assured of God's loving presence makes one keen to make the most of it in one's own life. So what should one pray for? Happiness? Yes, but happiness understood in a particular way. Geoffrey Elton, the Tudor historian, wrote, 'The recognition that happiness is not a right nor its pursuit a suitable ambition for any human being marks the move from adolescence to full adulthood.'[6] In the sense that Elton is thinking of happiness, this is true. Happiness is not only impossible but actually unreal, if it is thought of as an undisturbed condition of relaxed contentment, or an unending succession of fulfilling and prosperous events. On the other hand, happiness as the condition that arises from knowing, loving and enjoying God forever is indeed what the Christian prays for and can confidently anticipate. Surely that is what God wishes for every creature, the enjoyment of life lived with him and in him. Indeed! Francis de Sales, Bishop of Geneva 1602–22, taught the necessity of prayer on this basis. 'Since prayer opens our minds to the brightness of divine light and our will to the warmth of heavenly love, nothing so purges our mind of ignorance and our will of evil desires; its sacred waters freshen the soul, wash away our imperfections, revive the flowers of our good desires and quench the thirst of our hearts' passions.'[7] That is happiness, but it comes about through fulfilling our purpose in searching for God, for whose society we are made.

So, yes, we pray that we may be true, act justly, live courageously, be given true discernment, grow in wisdom and understanding, be true to our faith, have sufficient wealth in the broadest sense to satisfy all our needs and obligations, and find joy in God's creation. Children pray for new bicycles, and the latest design of mobile phone; we might pray for a pools win, a Gucci handbag, a ticket to the FA Cup Final, the last night of the Proms, or the survival of good local bookshops. Honesty is the best policy, so if that is what we want, we had better pray for it. But such petitions should be in the context of an awareness of the overarching love of God for each and every person and his whole world. And threats are impossible – 'God, if you don't give me what I ask for, then I shall not believe in you any more!'

Actually such requests are an expression of the fact that we have little faith, and less understanding of God. They are, by the same token, opportunities to think through again our understanding of what it is for God to be God and the way he wills that human life is to be lived. Paul writes to the Philippians, 'Rejoice in the Lord always; again I will say, Rejoice. Let your gentleness be known to everyone. The Lord is near. Do not worry about anything, but in everything by prayer and supplication with thanksgiving let your requests be made known to God. And the peace of God, which surpasses all understanding, will guard your hearts and your minds in Christ Jesus.'[8] If we live thankfully, make the best of our circumstances, and offer our prayers in this spirit, then God will keep us in the Body of Christ. Part of sharing in the school of prayer is that we learn good habits and work hard to bring our desires into line with what we say we believe about the world and God.

Part of genuine faith is the intention to bring others into conversation with God, and therefore to want good for them. This can begin with the realization that the way we are choosing to make use of the world is deleterious to the well-being of others. The world is most enjoyable, but we will only be enjoying it sensibly, let alone with proper respect, if our enjoyment is consistent with everyone else enjoying it too. Take tourism – seeing the world is great fun, often! However, if greater tourism brings cheap hotels, pollution, the end of local community life, the destruction of the environment and the proliferation of tawdry cultural values, then praying for local communities' well-being may conflict with our prayers for an enjoyable holiday. Inward investment may be good for us if we are fortunate enough to be one of the investors, but if we are one of those who are dispossessed because we can no longer afford to live decently in our home locality, it may be catastrophic.

Wanting to wish others well is a matter, first, of learning how best to enable them to live the life they have chosen for themselves; this may well require some reconsideration of how we are choosing to behave. We are called to love as God loves; the truth of the gospel as declared by God in Christ is that we can. Of course, only too frequently a response to what we perceive to be the needs of others is that we try to take over the responsibilities and duties of God and decide to do others good: in the face of ingratitude we then turn on God and blame him for our failure to live up to our own false ambitions. We need to remember that we are free to be what we are called to be, that is, creatures encouraged to do God's will. We are in fact free to be of service to others. Von Balthasar puts it like this: 'Man is indeed called to love, but only in a manner that permits him to live to the full his condition as a creature. He not only may, but must, strive for the highest degree of love; but this highest degree must be accompanied by the most complete realization of his true state as creature.'[9] We may not be able to solve all the world's problems, but since we are responsible for some of them there will always be something that we can do to make things a little better.

De Caussade anticipated the ennui and powerlessness that follows from too much exposure in the media to suffering and violence.[10] 'It's beyond us; it's outside my control. There's nothing I can do,' we say. But de Caussade is clear; given that the world is God's there is always something we can do, and if we set ourselves to identify it and to do it, we will have fulfilled the dominical command, 'Be perfect, therefore, as your heavenly Father is perfect.'[11] Our Lord would not have given us such a command, he argues, if we were always and everywhere incapable of fulfilling it. Thus look at the world in which you find yourself and ask what you can do, and do it. You cannot feed the entire world's hungry or end all wars? True, but do you owe a letter to a grandparent? Then in praying for her, write the letter you have been intending to write for months. Is a neighbour in hospital without visitors? Then in praying for his health, remember to visit him. When praying for good relations between Muslims and Christians, remember to learn more about Islam, and at least to smile when a Muslim enters your shop and asks to buy some writing paper. It is possible.

When we engage in conversation 'in secret', that is, silently in our hearts, we are, as I have said, nevertheless praying in community and in the presence of God. The conversation is divine, global, inclusive and powerful. Participation in God's conversation with his world encourages our hope because it instantiates in our words the reality that we aspire to, and the perfection or true happiness for which we long and to which we are naturally inclined. Augustine Baker, a seventeenth-century Benedictine monk, has matters in proper order when he talks of prayer as a duty of an internal contemplative life in his justly entitled 'Holy Wisdom'. '[Prayer is the activity] by which and in which alone we attain to the reward of all our endeavours, the end of our creation and redemption – to wit, union with God, in which alone consists our happiness and perfection.'[12] He talks quite rightly of duty, but of course the duty is a delight and a proper expression of our creaturely freedom.

Francis de Sales, when instructing Philothea to practise mental prayer (that is, personal prayer), tells her that 'unfortunately it is a lost art in our age'.[13] The same could surely be said of our own time, notwithstanding the huge amount of interest in spirituality, most of which, as far as I can see, is oblivious to the reality of God. So we need some help, as de Sales suggested. What help is there? There is the body of writing to be found on the spiritual life. The list here is endless and should be drawn on in as catholic a spirit as possible. No prejudice should lead us to eschew looking at and trying out anything and everything that might help us. We do not have to finish what we have started: if it does not help us, let's give it up and try something else. There is plenty to work at; we will never come to the end of it. It is sensible to remember, after all, that the purpose of spiritual reading is to become a better and more faithful person; it's true that in reading attentively we will learn things that we did not know, but that is not its primary purpose. And in any case little of it is permanently rewarding. Some things will be useful at one time of life, and others at another; only a few things will live with you for ever.

Examples of useful material are easy to produce. Have a look at the Early Church Fathers; they are often concerned with prayer and the spiritual life. Indeed, attention to them has been a springboard for reform at every period of Church history, for example, Methodism and the Oxford Movement. Augustine has sermons and commentaries on which we can draw as well as his *Confessions*; the Middle Ages have much to offer, whether we turn to Benedict, Aquinas, Bonaventure, *The Cloud of Unknowing* or Margery Kempe. And who would want to neglect St John of the Cross, Julian of Norwich, or Theresa of Avila? Everybody should try dipping into John Wesley, that restless polymath and roaming preacher of the eighteenth century, and read Charles Wesley's hymns – or at least more than the few familiar ones out of the six thousand or so that he wrote. And then there is Newman, G. K. Chesterton, W. H. Vanstone, Kenneth Leech and Neville Ward, the latter a man deeply read in literature and experienced in counselling persons who sought to practise the life of faith. And let's not forget either the vast tradition of spirituality bound up with Eastern Orthodoxy in its many forms. Olivier Clement is a most inspiring representative, who embodies respect for the tradition on which he draws with many contemporary insights.

There will inevitably be times when little of it makes sense and one is inclined to give it all up and sleep in front of the small screen! At such times it is sensible to take a step backwards, remember that one need never be alone, rely on the conversation of the faithful and draw on the wisdom of the generations. Nothing that is wise and true becomes redundant, though it may temporarily be in the background and fall into desuetude because it is unfashionable or because the present generation has forgotten how to make use of it. Since the purpose of prayer and of spiritual reading is to help us to remember God and give him our undivided attention it does not matter where the new spark of inspiration comes from which gets us going again. It may come about as a result of sharing in a celebration of the Eucharist, from attention to the Bible, from a novel or a poem, from reading a recommendation of a friend or returning to something familiar. For myself, John's Gospel, *The Cloud of Unknowing*[14] and de Sales' *The Devout Life* can be most useful at such times.

But there are other aids, variously enjoyed or abjured by the different traditions. I mention the rosary first because I imagine that there will be those who regard it as most helpful, while others will regard it as anathema. 'Isn't it concerned with the Virgin Mary? We have nothing to do with her; we believe in Christ!' I remember a Catholic friend of mine at Cambridge saying to me how much he was looking forward to being with me when I entered heaven. (He always was optimistic, which was good!) He thought I would be welcomed by Christ who would introduce me to the Lady beside him with the words, 'My mother, Kenneth. I don't believe you've met her!' It is good to remember that one of the finest books ever written on the rosary is by a Methodist minister, Neville Ward.[15] The rosary is *felt* prayer; as the good beads go through our hands and we recognize the sorrows and joys of Mary, we sense yet again the presence of God. Why ignore such an encouraging opportunity if it is there and if some find it so helpful?

Icons, pictures, images and signs, all have their place; they are expressions of lived experience. Let's consider them in turn. To walk into an Orthodox church in Greece, and find oneself surrounded by the saints, and in the presence of Christ whose feet are firmly placed on the ground behind the altar, whose arms embrace the community and whose face looks down from the heavens of the dome, is quite an experience. Look at Duccio's tryptych *The Virgin and Child with Saints*, dated 1315, now in the National Gallery, London. Are you not amazed by the expression of the Virgin? She gazes at – and almost through and around – the child Jesus in her arms. She is surrounded by prophets and saints, from eternity, both BC and AD; we are included in her world and invited by her, it seems to me, to pray for ourselves and for the world. John Drury points out that Duccio manages in the attitude of Mary to let us see Jesus as her Son *and* her Lord.[16]

The crucifix is an image proudly present in Catholic churches and many Christian homes. It draws us to share in the work of Christ through presenting the suffering and inspiring the hope of salvation. Our traditions, Catholic and Protestant, differ about whether the image of the cross should be empty and explicitly declare the victory won over death, or whether the crucified body should be represented. Is it a matter of taste? I think not; it is a matter of theology and worth engaging with. There is, of course, room for both, but neither should be taken for granted: it would be inappropriate to pass by on the other side. Lastly the physical making of the sign of the cross in blessing by the minister or priest, or by ourselves at grace before meals, or when receiving the bread and wine at Holy Communion, is a sign of the Word in action. To be blessed is to receive a sign of God's presence, and to be assured of his going with us.

Some Christians make retreats regularly, once or twice a year. They will go to favourite places, often joining resident communities where, for a few days, they can lose themselves totally in the business of practising the faith. A silent retreat is a special experience. One opens one's mouth only to praise God, and the reality of community is such that at mealtimes no one ever has, in my experience, even to ask for the pepper.

There may be some addresses, though when the speaker is good, they only serve to refresh one's spirit and remind one of those things that matter most.

Now not everyone will enjoy everything; no one should attempt to do everything. But the Church, the school of faith in which we try to enter into conversation with God, to encourage and be encouraged by one another, has resources on which we can and should draw. At the root of all, however, there is God and one another. Talking with God through appropriation of the language of faith is vital if we are to grow in faith. But talking with God will only bear fruit in our lives if we talk things out with one another. And how frequently do we do this? Perhaps we are embarrassed to share our faith, perhaps we are insecure in it, and perhaps we have not thought it through clearly for ourselves. But that is the point: we shall only think it through for ourselves if we do so with others, not just by attending the worship of the Christian community, or even by sharing in the celebration of the Eucharist. We have to engage with one another in sorting out what it means for our living in the world.

I suggested above just how hard the Early Church had to work to get itself into a position where it could live hopefully *in* the world, as opposed to simply waiting for the return of Christ, or trying to extract itself from the world. Our conversation with one another has to reflect this experience that is as vital for us as it was for them. We have some idea of what God is about in creating and committing himself to its perfection. So, what do we do about the homeless? What do we think about the new commission that the Pope has established to consider the use of condoms if there is the risk of transmitting AIDS? Should there be a ban on cheap air flights because of the dangers to the environment? Did Jesus really rise from the dead? What do we mean when we say that Jesus *physically* rose from the dead? Can one know God in this life? Have you ever forgiven anyone? How could you learn to want God more? What would it mean for you and for others if you did?

Conversation among ourselves, as a believing community in which we try to include the world we fear, and the people we suspect, will demand all the resources that the Christian tradition can muster. Of course, if we do not engage in the conversation we shall deplete even further what the Anglican report *Commission on Urban Life and Faith*, calls 'faithful capital'. That would be a disaster, not simply for the Church but for society at large which so obviously depends on it if it is to flourish. The reason for this is that without an awareness of God and participation in conversation with him, our humanity is diminished. J. B. Phillips wrote a book many years ago called *Your God is Too Small*. We need a new volume: *Our Vision of Humankind is Too Small*. We had better set about the task of talking with and not just about God with some enthusiasm, and believe that we shall succeed in learning to hope. This is real lifelong learning: it does not issue in the proliferation of certificates, but in the transformation of lives.

The best thing about the theme of this chapter is, you will have noted, that there is not an atom of originality about it; how could there be? What would be the point? Since God is the origin of all things, originality belongs to God alone. But having recalled God to mind and set about the task of praying personally in the Spirit, we have to learn also how to bring the world into our conversation. As Thomas Aquinas says, 'the consideration of creatures is useful in building up our faith'.[17] So let's turn to that now.

7

Conversation with Creation: Our Physical Environment

There was a time when it was thought that human being was the subject of a special creation by God; humankind was unconnected with the rest of the natural world over which, indeed, it had been given dominion by God himself. Nothing to worry about then! The world in which humankind is placed has been handed over to humankind by God to do with it whatsoever we fancy for our own benefit. Many philosophers and thinkers about morality criticize this profligate attitude, and blame the Jewish, Christian and Muslim traditions for our present environmental problems. John Passmore, for example, regards the Christian position as unreasonable because of its essential man-centredness. He quotes Calvin's confidence that God 'created all things for man's sake', and points out that what we now know of the evolution of life makes such a view obviously wrong.[1]

Passmore believes that Christian theology is irredeemable for the same reasons.[2] He acknowledges its flexibility but is suspicious that it can transform itself into something of empirical value. It may make of nature a sacred sphere, and want now to treat it with some respect, but he says that Christian theology cannot take account of current understandings of the world that arise from scientific enquiry and remain true to itself. I presume Richard Dawkins, that elegant writer on evolution, memes and genes, would take a similar view, though he argues that his position does nothing to undermine life's specialness.[3] Indeed, some of the discussion of intelligent design, a misnomer for a contemporary restatement of creationism, would suggest that there is truth in Passmore's accusation. The theory asserts the truth of a theological view on the process of creation independently of any evidence that scientific enquiry might throw up.

However, Passmore is wrong; there is much more to be said about the potential role of Christian theological enquiry and its dynamic nature. It is not in control disseminating indubitable divinely revealed truths, it is much more useful – it is a necessary and potentially illuminating partner in public debate. As a matter of fact, Christian theology is not, as Passmore suggests, man-centred, but God-centred. Christian theology can therefore only be true to itself *if* it engages fully in questioning and developing conversation with all disciplines of human enquiry, especially including the scientific and the technological. Christian theology, like the God to whom it bears witness, is incarnate: it only makes sense if we employ it *in via*, as we make our way through life, as a race and as persons.

The essential claim of Christian theology is that there is one world to which God has committed himself, whose physical aspects present a very complex set of inter-related processes of which the human species is itself an evolving subset. The benefits and intriguing questions that have arisen from human enquiry about the world are amazing; they have not only transformed the quality of life for the majority but resulted in a transformation of human self-understanding. Indeed, it could be argued that a crucial aspect of the opportunities now placed in human hands as the result of our own exploration of our environment is that humankind is now in control of its evolution to a degree and an extent only rarely considered previously.[4] The prospect may sweep us away with unfounded optimism or depress us with hellish visions. Actually, I suspect the future is neither heaven nor hell on earth. What in fact we shall have to do is discover how to manage our own future so that human being can prevail. Since this is exactly what the Christian faith suggests is God's purpose in creating, we shall in fact be learning to live so as to make a reality of the hope that is within us. Learning to hope is what all human life is about.

This is a dimension of the exciting work of the James

Martin Centre for Science and Civilization established in 2004 at Oxford University. It is located interestingly at the Said Business School with the purpose of researching the future, on a ten to one hundred-year timescale. James Martin, whose generosity lies behind the project, discussed in the 1970s, at the beginning of the development of information technology, such innovations as cellular telephones, the internet, the world wide web, instant messaging and telecommuting, every one of which has had a huge impact on society locally and globally. Further innovations in materials science, biotechnology, nanotechnology and chemical engineering will – not just may – change the way in which we think about human nature and the human person.

Christian theology has some work to do if it is to make the sort of contribution that I think it can uniquely make to human flourishing and which I believe it has the resources and freedom to offer. The experience of many is that the Christian imagination has indeed run out of puff. It seems more focused on saving relics than building new futures; more interested in defining truth than in investigating it; more concerned to protect buildings and institutions than to risk contributing to public conversation; less interested in finding out about the way research is going; and more concerned to speak out against the future. Canute would have been proud of us!

Not everything about science or what is believed about its prospects is hunky-dory, of course, but a blinkered approach to the excitement of scientific enquiry and the technological developments that will flow from it is extremely boring and irrelevant to what is already happening. Fortunately God gave us minds and affections we can employ in building pictures of our possible worlds based upon the very best available information: we have to bring all the resources we have at our disposal to bear upon the responsible task of choosing between them so that the world of human persons may flourish in relation to God and God's creation.

A *sine qua non* of all intelligent enquiry is that one must love the *subject* of one's enquiring. The purpose of scientific research, as of all enquiry, is to release the potential within the process under investigation and apply the knowledge gained in fruitful directions. Without a love of the subject and a desire to understand it, one will not 'hear' what the subject is saying in response to our questions, that is, our experiments. If, on the other hand, the focus is on 'forcing nature to deliver its secrets' in order to exploit and dominate nature, the underlying attitude of contempt for the *object* of one's study will lead to closing down the range of enquiry in order to get quick results: the outcome will be incomplete and cheap, of value only in the short term. It's one of the most fascinating aspects of the James Martin Institute, focused as it is on understanding likely long-term development, that it is based in the Said School of Business, since business is an aspect of life that is more usually associated with short-term benefit. The disastrous consequences of short-termism in contrast with long-term value can be seen, for example, in the notorious Enron case or indeed the willingness of so many to borrow extravagantly against a rapid rise in property prices. The mark of this blinkered approach is to be found in a focus on today's share value as opposed to investment in research and development. A due-diligence exercise is necessary when buying shares – in anything!

The fact is that the world in which Christians see themselves to be a responsible participant is one that God loves; this puts a secure foundation under sensitive enquiry and responsible judgement. We humans, created in the image of God, are called in partnership with God to love the world, to give ourselves to its study and through proper application of our knowledge to bring it to the next stage of evolutionary development, which if successfully accomplished will be a stage nearer to perfection. Not, of course, *to* perfection: there are no Utopias. Heaven on earth is a mirage no matter how frequently and earnestly announced! Nevertheless the range of possible futures over which we have been given power to judge is huge and continues to grow; we must not be limited in our enquiries by ignorance, prejudice or fear. Every possible future will have implications for human flourishing; each offers possible human improvement and the enhancement of human life. We have hardly yet begun to imagine what biotechnology and nanotechnology could offer us by way of increased prosperity, health and longevity.

God has given himself to his creation so that it may be perfected through the willing co-operation and affectionate commitment of humankind who is made in his image. Aquinas understood this and, as we saw at the close of the last chapter, reckoned that the consideration of creatures would be useful for the building up of faith. He gave four reasons for this. First, through meditating on God's works we would be able to admire and consider the divine wisdom. Second, through consideration of his wisdom, we would admire his power, and therefore find ourselves wanting to reverence God in our hearts. Third, we would be inflamed with the love of God's goodness; and fourth we should find ourselves becoming aware of our likeness to the divine perfection.[5] I shall consider each of these points in turn.

First, meditating on God's works will enable us to admire and pay attention to God's wisdom. It will, but surely only if the investigator takes to his enquiry a faith in God and his creative will? Even if this were true, it does not disprove the truth or value of Christian theological reflection. It is, of course, impossible to *deduce* the fact of a Creator from an examination of the creation; William Paley was in error when he sought to apply the analogy of the intricacies of the watch and the watchmaker to the complexities of the natural world and the existence of a Creator.[6] The cosmological argument for the existence of God is invalid, as an argument. However, the fact that the world exists is a mystery that cries out for an explanation; the proposal of the Christian tradition that it is the continuing work of a God who has committed himself to its success is worth working at. Indeed, there are heuristic arguments in favour of the view that were we to take Christian theological enquiry seriously we would improve not only our desire to engage with the world so as to understand it, but the quality of the judgement that informs the ways in which we make use of our knowledge.

Thus, I consider Anthony Flew's review of his position and consequent acceptance of the idea of a Creator to be interesting, as also Paley's analogy, since they at the least take seriously a notion of Creator. However, since their approaches offer no insight into the character of the Creator they seem to have no practical value. The Christian tradition, however, does just that; it offers an account of the character of the Creator, by describing the manner of his personal, creative activity as 'redemptive'. God, as Christians view him, makes and remakes his world so that it remains fit for purpose, namely the fulfilment of personal life as expressed in human being. Christian theology embodies the belief that the Creator is wholly responsible for the world, omniscient, omnipotent and all-loving, and that he is committed to making a success of his work in partnership with humankind. This set of beliefs provides a frame of reference, which encourages an affectionate and optimistic attitude to the world, of which humankind is a part, and nourishes genuinely creative judgement about how it could be developed.

It is not vacuous either; not every judgement about technological innovation is consistent with such a view. For example, we know how important it is that new drugs are tested finally on human subjects but it is a necessary condition that the human subject is a volunteer. Volunteers may need to be paid; that would not be an objection in itself. However, if the money involved were so great as to be likely to persuade some people, against advice and their own judgement, to act contrary to their own best interests, that would be wrong. Furthermore, if deception were employed in obtaining volunteers, or only those serving a prison sentence were approached, or only persons in remote parts of the world who were unlikely to be of interest to the media, there would be serious grounds for concern. The new drug, the result of intelligent enquiry and careful experiment, is for the benefit of all; to compromise that by in principle *requiring* some to 'volunteer' and not others would be contrary to a Christian view of God's relation with the world, and the role of human beings in working with God for its perfection. It would, I agree, be contrary to many moral principles. However, I would wish to argue at greater length than there is space for here that moral goodness in human affairs is rooted in the goodness of the Creator, the source of all perfections.[7]

Meditating on God's works involves loving the world, recognizing one's relationship with it in all its dimensions, and attending to it in all its complex interest and fascination. 'Meditating' is not, however, just a matter of 'thinking about' the world, it includes thinking 'with' the world, that is, somehow 'getting inside it'. One way of getting at this point is to refer to the familiar remark of Kepler who spoke of 'thinking God's thoughts after him'. And Einstein wrote that it was with the help of natural science that the thoughts of God may be tapped and grasped. Indeed, Friedrich Dürrenmatt once said, 'Einstein used to speak of God so often that I almost looked upon him as a disguised theologian.'[8] I would not wish to push the analogy too far, but certainly an approach to the business of scientific enquiry that assumes that there is dialogue at its heart, that we are *talking* with the subject of our enquiry and trying to listen to its intelligible responses is important both to our acquisition of genuine knowledge and to a proper understanding of our place in the world.

Humankind, as Christian theology understands it, will find its true nature by co-operating with God in order to share with him in the fulfilment of his purpose in creation. The wisdom of God is manifest in the fact that we have the mind to engage with his creation, the capacity to share its growth pangs, the ability to make sensible judgements and to review them in the light of experience. There is nothing obvious about this: the truth does not stare us in the face. How could it be so? For if it were perfectly obvious and we could read the answers off, as it were, on an autocue, we should lack the freedom to enquire, and therefore the freedom to know God and become ourselves. The wisdom of God is implicit in the very process alluded to above. We take to the world an understanding of God, his character and purpose, but have to give it flesh by the ways in which we approach the study of his world and the way in which as a result we come to think of ourselves as students in the school of faith.

Aquinas' second point is that consideration of creatures leads us to admire the supreme power of God and begets in our hearts a reverence for God. Our temptation, I suggest, in the face of indifference, ignorance and misunderstanding is to take over the job ourselves. Many a manager has failed to respect the qualities of a junior, and eschewed the important task of educating him or her. In the 1980s, the Thatcher government had an inner-city initiative, the purpose of which was to renew that desolate environment. I happened to visit Toxteth at the time and noticed the plans to renovate this extremely run-down area of Liverpool. The plans looked good on paper but lacked one essential dimension – the involvement of the local community.

It was a racially mixed community with high unemployment, poorly educated and with a high crime rate; the assumption was that it had little or nothing to offer. So there was no consultation with the local population. The important thing was to get on with the job, improve the neighbourhood, renovate the houses, plant trees and establish some social infrastructure. Those employed on the job were for the most part brought into the area and accommodated in temporary buildings erected on the site. Things did not go well and recriminations soon began. The government felt that it was unappreciated – all this public money was being spent on doing the local people some good and this was the thanks they got for their trouble! The local population felt that they were not being treated as persons with ideas and visions of their own. Indeed they were not even doing the work! They were just pawns in someone else's political game. The intentions were very good, but the means employed to put the policies into effect were unwise. We can see now the lack of wisdom; yet we do not learn and still wish in many contexts to take over and pursue a policy of revolution rather than evolution.

In contrast, let's look at the creating with which God is engaged. God's purpose is to enable persons to flourish through growing in knowledge of the opportunities implicit in their situation, and in relationship with one another. He does not abandon them to their fate, but commits himself to making a success of his world by sharing it with them. In the face of difficulty, however, he does not rush in and do the job himself for the simple reason that to do so would be an admission of failure. Instead of succeeding in creating persons capable of living their own lives and making their own unique contribution to the perfecting of his purpose, all he would have done was make automatons, whose predetermined lives would be put into place like the colours and shapes on a painting-by-numbers picture. Happily God demonstrates his power by showing that he has power over himself to enable the freedom of the world he is making. Such courtesy and attention to his creation surely begets in our hearts a reverence for him. He is faithful who promised. Our learning about and with the world is grounded in the quite proper hope we have in God.

Third, reverence for God does not mean that we spend our time on our knees with eyes downcast in fear and trembling of the Almighty. Quite the contrary! Consideration of the creature leads us to see just what opportunities are before us, and to recognize that they are God-given opportunities, not ones we have constructed for ourselves or which have emerged accidentally as a result of our own hard-won knowledge and skill. The wisdom and power of God, which we intuit as a result of considering the creature, means that we can quite properly see that God saw that his world was good. In contemporary management-speak, we might say that God saw to it that the world he was making was fit for purpose; or perhaps, in simple human terms, that we realized that the world was on our side. So while we would be wrong to imply, as apparently Calvin did, that the world had been created by God for our benefit in any sense that suggests we have a right to plunder it with indifference, it would be right to say that the world of which humankind is an evolving dimension is able to provide everything that is necessary for real human life. Persons can flourish in a God-given environment; the presence of the living Christ declares the truth of this.

So of course we can love God as the source of all goodness, and set about the task of studying the world, coming to terms with our circumstances and taking delight in the vast divine creativity in which we share. No wonder that the fourth implication of considering the creature is for Aquinas that we begin to see what it means to be 'in the image of God', that humankind can sense a certain likeness to the divine perfection. This astonishing, apparently outrageous claim is the nub of the Christian gospel. In fulfilling our calling to be human creatures in relation with one another, the world and God we have already begun to enjoy the fruit of our hope, we are learning to hope. The world of which we are a dimension is free not determined, open not closed, life-giving not life-denying. We can therefore look at it with love, and expect to be loved back, in the sense that if we engage it in creative conversation we shall find that we are in conversation with God, the Redemptive-Creator with whom we are able to work in partnership.

The idea that humankind is created in the image of God has been the occasion of much debate. The Early Church Fathers for the most part regarded it as referring to the Son of God, for, as they thought, the Fall implied mere man could not share the image of God in any real sense. Part of the significance of baptism was that it restored in the person the image of God. Augustine presented a different point of view when he declared the soul to be modelled upon the Trinity in memory, understanding and will. The most disastrous perspective was offered by the Reformers who asserted the total depravity of man and the total erasure of the image of God. We have to come alive again to the ever-present reality of God in his commitment of himself to the world's, and therefore to human, well-being. As we might say, what God has joined, let no man put asunder. Rahner is right: there is no such thing as ungraced nature nor, therefore, any such thing as ungraced human nature. We can, therefore, through contemplation of the creature begin to discern the reality of God's presence, and dimly begin to see in ourselves, in our humanity, the image of God. Thank God!

If this approach is correct, then neither theology nor science can independently provide complete accounts of the human condition. Scientism is simply an attempt to define the knowledge derived by the use of the scientific method as the only knowledge open to human enquiry. It does not work. In like manner a theology that takes no account of the world and thinks it can simply declare so-called revealed truths is equally obscurantist; let's call it theologism. Scientism and theologism are false views of the world.

It is sometimes suggested that a fundamental distinction between science and theology is that science makes progress, whereas theology cannot. Scientific enquiry will, of course, always be able to make progress because the application of the methods of science raise new questions hitherto unrecognized. That's true; some of the questions that science is now tackling have only arisen as the result of earlier successful research. Astronomers did not conceive of black holes until observations and subsequent developments in theoretical physics had suggested they might exist; now they are the subject of keen study. The investigation of the genetic code, now an area of huge interest to geneticists and medical research, has only come about as the result of the imaginative interpretation of information about DNA. However, the changing *understanding* of the world that we gain from the successful experimental application of scientific methods and the imaginative interpretation of the results does not bring into question the fundamental reality or existence of the world that is being studied. The world is dynamic, always active and in flow.

The success of the scientific enterprise as its techniques of investigation change and the range of intellectual disciplines increases will, however, naturally give rise to questions about the nature of science itself, which will qualify and shape our account of it. Just what is the ground on which successful scientific judgement is based? What is it to enquire scientifically? What in fact are the methods of scientific enquiry?

But these productive features of scientific enquiry are equally to be found in theology: in the light of experience it too shifts its assumptions, changes and develops its methods of enquiry, and as a result comes up with revised conclusions. Newman tried to come to terms with the process of which he became personally conscious because of changes in his own position on the faith: he entitled his book *Essay on the Development of Christian Doctrine.*[9] On the occasion of the publication by John Robinson, the notable Bishop of Woolwich, of *Honest to God*, the *Observer* newspaper printed an article with the headline, 'Our Image of God Must Go'.[10] Though I believe Robinson was unhappy with the title, which was the work of a sub-editor, it fairly represents a proper approach to theology. Neither God as we understand the reference of the term, nor theology, are like Blackpool through a stick of rock; they do not go in at one end of enquiry and come out the same at the other!

At a time when human perception of the natural world was peopled by powers and spirits, and when there was little understanding that could remotely be called scientific, it may have been appropriate to think of God as a more powerful spirit who could control the elements and protect one when in danger. Getting on the right side of God might then have seemed the most rational thing to do. But once science has begun to change one's idea of the world, one's idea of God will change also. Hence the quite proper influence on theological understanding of later developments, of Darwin and evolutionary theory, Freud and self-knowledge, Durkheim and sociology, Watson and Crick and the unravelling of DNA, the internet and the world wide web. Changes in the way we understand and talk of God in the light of experience do not imply that God has changed, any more than changes resulting from scientific enquiry about the world mean that the world has changed. Indeed, for there to be any such thing as a growing knowledge and appreciation of the nature of the world or God, we must assume, as we do, that each remains consistent.

But also, as with scientific method, we have come to question our understanding of the nature of theological enquiry itself. The progressive development of our understanding of the world through the sciences is impressive, but, given what Christians believe about the nature of the Creator and the role of humankind in creation, not actually surprising. Likewise our changed understanding of what it is for God to be God, which has followed from developments in our understanding of the human relationship with the world, is not surprising either. If one changes, so should the other;

each grows and adapts in conversation with the other. They are not after all, two quite independent languages; they constitute one symbiotic attempt to hold together our understanding of God and God's world of which humankind is a part. Both are the lively work of the imagination, by which, in the light of careful attentiveness to the nature of things and the disciplined exercise of reason, humankind seeks to find its place in the world.

So what does this theological approach to our human experience offer by way of help or encouragement in the light of the many problems with which we are faced? Let's suppose the theology we have briefly outlined is true. This world is the creation of a good God, who has seen to it that the world that we inhabit is good; that is, it is capable of providing everything necessary for human flourishing. Does this help? If we actually believe it, it will mean at the very least that in the face of difficulty there is no need to panic. It will also mean that while we may not be able to solve the problems, there will always be things to discover that will bring about an improvement. Of course, since the future is in our hands, we will need to direct our enquiries in the right directions and make the right choices when the opportunity arises. So let's look with embarrassing brevity at four of the fundamental problems that we face.

We are short of energy. The problem is serious because industry depends upon it, as do our systems of communication, from trains and planes to the world wide web. Our civilization will collapse without it. So what can we do? No answer can be deduced from the Bible because it is not a textbook of science and technology. But is it true that we are short of energy? Well, not really; what we are short of is oil – experts tell us that we have at the most 20 to 30 years left if we do nothing about it and demand continues to grow at the present rate. But we could be more efficient in its use. And there are geologists who reckon that there are vast untapped resources of oil, which it will be profitable to exploit as and when the price rises. Perhaps we are more worried about our western security of supply than that the world will run out of oil. As an American comedian said about Iraq, 'What I can't work out, is why our oil got under their sand!' But in any case we are not confined to oil if what we want is energy. There's enough wind in Kansas to provide the whole of the USA with energy. Wind and wave power, if harnessed, could supply much of the UK's needs. And there is always the marvellous potential benefit locked up inside the atom that offers inexhaustible supplies of energy. None of these will of themselves solve the problem. I say the problem, but is it technical, political, social, economic? Surely, all these; every problem is multifaceted.

More serious than the supply of energy is the availability of water. Depending on where you live in the world, there seems to be abundance, or none at all. Parts of Africa are suffering from a drought so serious that cattle, people and crops are dying from starvation. China is chronically short of water and the situation is getting worse. Already one third of the country is desert. The water table in California, built up over hundreds of years, has depleted by a third in the last 50; and the water table in India has got so low in places that it is contaminated by salt water.

Recourse to dam-building offers no panacea. Dams under construction in China and India will dispossess several million people. The Narmada Dam in north-west India, for example, which began as an attempt to provide both irrigation to a large Dalit community and generate electricity for a city population and industrial development, has come more and more to focus on the needs of business and to neglect those of peasant fishing and agriculture. It is not surprising, because the government needs prosperous industry to provide employment and meet the needs of a growing urban population. Industry provides the necessary tax if public services are to be maintained and disorder avoided. Many of the dispossessed Dalits have been removed to places without housing, medical services or prepared opportunity for agriculture. Water redistribution is not easy, though attention to the difficult tasks of improving the 'harvesting', storing and distribution of water would be helpful. The situation is serious; failure to resolve the issues threaten international peace as a state upstream dams a river and denies the state downstream the benefits on which it has hitherto relied. But we can at least say, as Christians, that any attempt to solve water shortages that does not from the beginning take into account human flourishing of all involved, is wrong, and will fail.

Global warming has been described as the most serious threat to the world. Glaciers in Europe and Iceland are melting, and the polar ice cap is receding. Sea levels are rising, with an increasing threat of flood in low-lying coastal areas mostly inhabited by some of the world's poorest people. Bangladesh would be an example. Violent weather conditions are increasing. The impact on agriculture will be profound, once again most deleteriously on the world's most impoverished countries. There has been much debate about global warming, whether it is really happening and if so what the causes are, but most experts now affirm its reality, its seriousness and that the cause is largely if not exclusively the result of human behaviour, most particularly the consequence of carbon emissions from burning fossil fuels. There have been several unsuccessful attempts to agree international policies to deal with it. But some countries, the USA in particular, have resisted because they believe it will be too expensive and threaten the prosperity of their economy. Some experts predict disaster and say that we have gone too far down the road to reverse a trend that is now built into the world's systems. But there is sufficient evidence that we could take steps to reverse the process over 50 years. We need tenacity, wider scientific enquiry and political will.

Lastly, population growth. The human population grows exponentially and threatens the balance of ecological systems. It is unnecessary to go into detail because it is clear from the costs of travel, the destruction of the natural world, the depletion of resources, and the piling up of human life in heaps in cities where over the next 50 or so years more than 70 per cent of the world's population will dwell. So what is to be done? It is not easy. President Putin of Russia has announced incentives to encourage population growth in the face of the current decline in birth rate of three-quarters of a million per annum. Western Europe has an ageing population, and who will do the work to ensure that the economy will continue to prosper? Will immigrants be employed, with the consequent changes in the nature of Western European society? We are beginning to see and feel the political dimensions of the questions facing us. And there are implications, too, for the balance of religious representation in an area. For example, one religious tradition may embrace birth control and another not, which could lead to a change in the balance of power between the two traditions. Could it be used as an instrument of policy where one tradition seeks to dominate the other? Islam and Christianity, for example?

These are all extremely difficult and complex matters: none of them has a simple solution. But despair is unwarranted and pointless. This is a world to which God is committed and which is good. The implication is that we can do something about them all, if we pay proper attention, identify the problems and begin to appreciate their complexity; accept their reality and stop denying their existence; stop pretending that they don't exist, believing that they will go away if we ignore them; and stop thinking that they will solve themselves – by the operation of the market, for example. In fact, we had better get down *together* to the business of making things better – for everyone! Of course, if we – that is you and I – treat the world as a goody-box and plunder it for our own benefit, and believe that we can get what we want and to hell with the rest, we shall all fail. It is possible to make of the world something of delight for everyone, though hard work will be necessary. We have something to learn from one another and we should look on one another in this light: fear of God, of the world and of one another will get us nowhere. It is actually contrary to the nature of things, for at the heart of this world's very being, as it is of God's Being, is love, and 'perfect love casts out fear'. Surely, we can learn to hope! The signs are there.

The openness of God to conversation and our ability to talk with the world in which we are set are important dimensions of the optimism that we should feel in the face of difficulty, but there is another – ourselves. Are we willing to converse with one another, to listen and to take seriously our many needs, concerns and interests into account? This human dimension of our environment is what I now turn to, for the future depends very largely on us. What do we want? What by our behaviour does it seem we are trying to get?

8

Conversation with the World: Our Human Environment

A key to understanding the role of the Christian community, the Church, as it works with God in the furtherance of his generous purpose in creating, is to recognize that the Church proleptically includes all people. The Church celebrates God's presence with his world; the Church offers to God in the Eucharist, on behalf of all people, the whole world of creation. All persons are of equal worth and symbolically given equal access to the world in the bread and wine that they share. But the fact of the *graced* character of all human nature has to be enjoyed and celebrated. Our sacramental sharing of God with the world, we have to understand, means that we are committed to making real the unity of all humankind and working for it with all our mind, and heart and soul. We must want to achieve it, and therefore be doing all in our power to establish in each person's experience the reality of what we *say* we believe in.

We are all one in Christ. Indeed we are, and there has been progress towards the realization of this vision even if we still have some way to go before 'all God's chillun got shoes'. It is not so long ago, in the 1930s I think, that Ella Fitzgerald was prevented from boarding a plane in Honolulu to make way for a white passenger. She was, of course, one of the most celebrated jazz performers of her time, but she was black. The fact that she was travelling first class with a maid and was on her way to fulfil an engagement in Australia made not the slightest difference; she was black. She was held up for three days but that didn't matter; she was black. Many times in her career she had to enter a hotel by the kitchen entrance and use the servants' staircase to get to her first-class suite, notwithstanding the fact that the hotel was, of course, prepared to accept her money. After all, black money is as valuable as white money, isn't it! It doesn't bear thinking about, but in the interests of truth and justice we had better think about it. It doesn't happen now, we say. Certainly things are better than they were for many people, though we know that further progress is necessary before we all feel one and at home together in God's world.

Slavery is a thing of the past. It was made illegal in Britain in 1808 and declared unconstitutional in the USA in 1865 at the close of the American Civil War. But it still exists. In the West the number of women illegally brought from Eastern Europe and 'sold' into the slavery of prostitution is huge and, so we are told, increasing. And we know that in some places in Africa and the Far East there is real slavery as well as embedded social relationships that amount to slavery even if they are not legally in that category. Come to think about it, there are many economic relationships between nations where the trading style of a dominant power threatens, if it does not totally remove, the freedom of another independent state. The World Trade Organization was established to try to deal with this issue; that is good, but it has not yet managed to deal with the overweening power of the prosperous nations so as to liberate the potential of the developing world.

Where do we stop? We can't. The position of women in many parts of the world is such that they are denied education, independence, property, or any voice in public life. Do we have to accept the treatment of women in some societies just because it is claimed to be a part of their religion, or their traditional way of life? Children in Sierra Leone and Uganda have been kidnapped, raped, forced to join in military activity, killed or maimed. The tedious repetition of what we think we know about the world's suffering – they don't have to keep on reminding us! – is such that we are inclined to pass by on the other side. The daily publication of new horrors in the media accustoms us to the terror of life for many, and encourages the thought that there is little if anything that we can do about it.

There are, of course, things that could be done. We don't know what exactly in the vast majority of cases, but I am encouraged by the faith to believe that there is no problem, careful attention to which will not reveal opportunities for improvement. So let's remember again what we are saying and doing when we share in the central act of Christian worship, the Eucharist. Christians make an offering of themselves in Christ on behalf of all people; in principle, in imagination and in hope, we stand with and alongside every other person, and remember for good each and every human life. The grace of Christ's gift of his Body that we receive in the bread and the wine is not just for those who are present, or those who are baptized, but for us all. The Protestant emphasis on the *me* is right in its proper place – 'Christ died for *me*' – but in fact we need to set it in context. Christ only gave his life for me because I am included in the *all* for whom he died. So what are we doing about sharing this divine gift with the world?

The actual distribution of the bread and the wine at the Eucharist is one of the most humbling experiences that any priest or minister can know. Hands outstretched, black, brown, white, yellow, injured, tired, worn, well-manicured, broken or dirty, each one is receiving God. Well, all right, if you do not like it put just like that, let's say that each worshipper on behalf of all is receiving assurance that everything necessary for salvation is available to him or her now, and for ever. Isn't that the same thing? And the priest, who is standing for the one and only celebrant, Christ, is the means whereby God is given. That is, come to think of it, not humiliating but awesome and hugely encouraging for us all, including the priest: the world has received God and is free to love him.

Tissa Balasuriya, a Sri Lankan priest, once said that to share in Holy Communion without doing anything to make a reality of the unity of humanity by working for human liberation, when you had just celebrated it, was tantamount to blasphemy.[1] The sad thing is that unless it is shared, the Real Presence becomes very unreal indeed. There is hardly any difference between such unlovely, unlively faith and no faith at all.

Such celebration obviously does not of itself solve the problems we face, but it does draw us back to the ground of our hope, God. We are one people, called by God to be his people and trying to share God with his world. In so doing we are doing what he wills and what it is possible to do. Each person is diminished by the enslavement of any other person; we shall only flourish as faithful persons to the extent that we welcome the whole world into the conversation of God with us. So the fact that the Church is universal, that there is no nation, race, age phase or gender that is not represented in its membership, is important. It is also vital to recall that there are persons involved in the Christian community drawn from every profession, educational experience, variety of skill and discipline of enquiry. Artists of every kind, painters, garden designers, sculptors, miniaturists, musicians, performers and creators are all involved. And let us not forget that we have to include every religious, philosophical and moral tradition of enquiry and indeed the good, the bad and the indifferent; all are proleptically and really involved in God's conversation with the world of humankind in which we are centrally involved. Pride is irrelevant here. As our Lord said to the woman taken in adultery, 'Let anyone among you who is without sin be the first to throw a stone at her.'[2] The story is not included in manuscripts of the Gospel until the third century, but it may well have been thought by the editor(s) to illustrate vividly the later remark of Jesus that John includes: 'You judge by human standards, I judge no one.'[3] Bearing witness to this fact is the testing task of a lifetime.

The truth of the gospel of Christ is not capable of being reduced to what has become known as political theology: Jesus was not a revolutionary, nor is the Christian gospel a substitute for a political creed. Nevertheless, Christian faith encourages political awareness and adds force to the importance of making astute and creative political judgements. The prayer for St Pancras Day is not worth the paper it is (not) written on! 'O God, the Father of all, keep me on the right track so that I remain in my proper station and do not go off the rails. Amen.' Change for the better is at the heart of the Christian political philosophy, always keeping in mind the fact that such change will be evolutionary and confirm continuities, links and opportunities rather than revolutionary disjunction.

Political authority, like the exercise of authority in any context including the Church, is consensual when it works: it is not simply a matter of doing what you are told. I remember Kenneth Grayston saying of the use of *akouein*, 'to hear', in the New Testament that listening is all very well, but if you don't understand what you have heard you will not be free to will what is good, only conditioned to act in accordance with what you have been told to do. God wants us to listen to the gospel, by which he means understand it and test our understanding as we live it out in our personal lives and engage in debate about the direction of public policy.

Every person is called to make a contribution to the public well-being; every person who is denied that opportunity by circumstances, or whose experience leads that person to believe that he or she has nothing to say, is unfree. One task of the Church, which as I have said proleptically includes all people, is to give a voice to the voiceless, and in this sense to be a stimulus to the maturing of political life. This will require listening carefully when the world is deaf to what is going on, but it will only rarely and exceptionally involve speaking in place of others; rather it means engaging in the more demanding task of helping the voiceless to speak for themselves.

Ask any teacher; nothing is more depressing than having someone in the class who assumes to answer for the student who after tremendous effort was just about to share his or her wisdom perhaps for the very first time. It may have been something important which, at least temporarily, limits the range of human conversation. The composer Nikos Skalkottas studied the violin in Athens, and composition under Weill and Schoenberg in Vienna. In 1933, still a young man, he returned to Athens where he died in 1949 at the age of 44. He earned his living as a back-desk violinist often earning his living by playing in cafés. Meanwhile, unknown to almost everyone, he put together a vast oeuvre of music, practically none of which was performed in his lifetime: indeed it was only in the 1960s that his genius began to be recognized. I do not know whether he sought obscurity so that he could do what he knew he had it in him to do – compose music – or whether it was the consequence of public indifference and deafness to his personal style. Certainly, nobody listened to him and as a result we missed his voice.

Whether we welcome it or not, we cannot deny the intimate unity of our one physical environment: a cigarette packet discarded in the West Indies is washed up on the west coast of Scotland; 20 years after an explosion in a nuclear plant in Chernobyl in the Ukraine, mountain pasture in North Wales remains contaminated. The interdependence of the world's ecosystems is common knowledge, but we seem to be able to adopt policies that ignore the fact that the world of human affairs is itself a primary actor within the world's ecosystem. To the extent that it is recognized policy-makers, constrained by the electorate, honour it in words rather than action: this cannot continue if human being is to flourish. The Church does not have to be persuaded of this, one would hope; it is a basic dimension of its faith. The whole creation is one.

So if, as we believe, the world is one, we will increasingly come to recognize the interdependence of human life, especially the performance of the world's economies; the performance of one depends upon the performance of all the others. The physical world, the socio-economic and cultural worlds of human experience, are obviously interdependent. We all share one weather system, one set of routes for international trade, one deposit of raw materials on which we draw for manufacturing. We compete for raw materials. Hence the growth of the economies of China and India puts pressure on the price of metals such as copper, and on oil, which exaggerated by the activity of speculators impacts on inflationary pressures in the developed economies of America, Japan and Western Europe. As population grows and adds to the pressure for jobs, employment will tend to move to those countries where wages are lowest, education and training soundly invested in, regulation of health and safety at work slight, and welfare costs kept to a minimum.

Many believe that all this plays into the hands of the multi-national corporations who exert too much power because in a very competitive global market no country has sufficient economic power to buck the trend. And it is all too easy for corporations now that they can switch capital, employment opportunity and technical know-how from one country to another at the click of a mouse.

The fact is, as we are beginning to appreciate in its raw truth, that however powerful a country is, economically or militarily or politically, there are forces that it cannot control and relationships that it cannot direct. The United States discovered this when it sent forces into Somalia; the USA with Britain and her allies are finding the same to be true in their dealings with Iraq and Iran; and the United Nations is discovering the same in the Sudan. Hence the emergence of regional groups such as the European Union; and the incipient coalition of political power in South America opposed to the domination of capitalism and intent upon the nationalization of energy supply. On the one hand this is a not inconsiderable threat since Venezuela, for example, probably has the second largest known oil deposits in the world. But regionalism will, no more than nationalism, build policies that support the human environment since it too is built upon a belief in the competitive advantage of nations. If we are all to enjoy the one God-given world in which we are set, co-operation and partnership must replace greed and private ambition. A natural competitive spirit characterizes human being, but to be useful it will be channelled to serve the common good. If we could learn to compete with one another in well-doing, what a different world we should enjoy. Such competition would be fertile ground in which to learn to hope.

Should we then as the Christian community fear globalization, set ourselves against it and try to reverse it? The question is ridiculous. Globalization is, in one form or another, here to stay; it is pointless to set ourselves against it. So let's join publicly in the world's conversation so that the opportunities implicit in globalization are made available to all. And they can be. We of all people can be sure of that, since it is of the essence of our faith that there is one God, one world, and one people. Globalization is natural territory for Christian faith. The purpose of God in creating is that persons may flourish. Nothing can or will prevail against that purpose. Our critique of all institutions, political parties, social programmes and economic policies must be grounded on this confidence. The fact that the world in principle, God's world, recognizes the truth of what we believe, means that we can work with enthusiasm and optimism so that the essential implication of globalization is actually worked out in the experience of all. If each is to succeed, all must succeed. No chain is stronger than its weakest, poorest, broken link.

The accusation is nevertheless frequently made that globalization will make humanity subservient to profit, domesticate education so that it provides fodder for the workplace, and lead inevitably to violent conflict as each nation, race, class and religion attempts to secure its own power in the face of imminent doom. In fact, some argue that the future threatens the survival of that essential sense of individual worth in personal relationship which every one of us knows for ourselves when we pause to remember what we value most in life. One could be forgiven for thinking that there is some truth in this. If systems, numbers and the con-tractual conditions informing remuneration replace persons in a doctor's surgery, then the person who is actually present will become invisible and the doctor incapable of doing his or her job. If a company's share value dominates boardroom conversation to the exclusion of attention to a company's living stakeholders, employees, pensioners, customers, sup-pliers – yes, and shareholders too – all of whom are consti-tuted of persons with lives, families, interests, concerns and contributions to make, then the glue that holds the organiza-tion together will fail. If a government's interest in the electorate is reduced to securing votes for the next election, then it will lose authority and become suspect as self-serving, focused on power rather than service, party rather than com-munity. This is true of government at all levels, and indeed of constitutional arrangements in every organization – church, tennis club or debating society. But 'it ain't necessarily so!' The human person will not fall into the background and wither away. It can only happen if we allow it to. The Christian community points powerfully to the strength of the human spirit as it lives its faith in practice and calls into question those persons, institutions, policies and economic processes that try to ignore human well-being.

The situation is hardly new. Human societies have always surrounded themselves with fears of one sort or another, sometimes focused on persons, sometimes on impersonal forces, almost always with exaggerated anxiety. And they have always grasped after phantasmagoria in an attempt to free themselves from illusory disaster – racial purity, a holy grail, Eldorado, a magic mushroom.[4] The human person has not yet succumbed; we will not be defeated in the future. Reason, imagination, common sense, courage, mutual loyalty, personal affection and hope have seen us through every apparent catastrophe. War, natural disaster, plagues, misunderstandings, misinterpretations of experience have all been absorbed into the life experience on which humans have continued to build their hope. Since the Christian faith is grounded in God, that is neither paradoxical nor surprising.

The power of the human person shines through in art in every generation, even in that darkest of centuries, the twentieth. Shostakovich wrote his Eighth Symphony in the middle of the Second World War; the first performance was in 1943. It is a bleak expression of the awfulness of war, and of the terrible suffering of the Russian people. After the passionate outpouring of the first movement, the last movement dies away not with a whimper but in the hopeful statement of a still, small voice; slight, insistent, intimate, personal. 'We shall overcome.' At least this is how I hear it. Francis Bacon, one of the greatest painters of the twentieth century, makes the human body into chunks of meat (*Study from the Human Body*, 1981), brings the 'inside' person outside (*Head VI*, 1949), and opens himself up to view in his amazing self-portraits (*Self Portrait*, 1978).[5] Here is what systems, powers and the desperate forces of indifference can threaten, but never actually achieve! You may not like his work, but as I see it Bacon is obsessed with what it is to be a self, and struggles to express the screams for freedom that are within us. Francis Bacon thus reveals the inextinguishable zest for life in every human life.

Even in basic political terms, it is simply marvellous that the human spirit cannot be extinguished. How else does one explain the liberation of South Africa from the tyranny of apartheid? The white government believed that it was undefeatable, notwithstanding the fact that for years its security had been on the edge of a precipice. They had money, land, education and political influence, they ran the army and the security services and controlled the business sector. They had gold, platinum and uranium, much desired commodities, not to mention others such as copper whose routes to international trade they commanded. What is more, they had the western powers on their side because in the Cold War with Russia the West relied upon the naval coaling facilities provided by the Simonstown Agreement. But nothing is for ever; ships became oil-powered, bigger and they stayed at sea longer and the South African coaling facilities lost their strategic importance. One by one the practical matter of international influence was dissipated and, thrown back on their own resources, they found the human desire for freedom too strong to resist. As Christian faith has it, the human spirit is invincible, not because it holds all the cards and can play to win, but because that is how things are in this world: the human person is king in a world made by God for just this purpose.

An analogous argument can be made in the case of the collapse of the Soviet Union and the emerging independence of the Baltic States and the countries of Central and Eastern Europe. Not that everything has been completed in one movement. Neither in Southern Africa nor in the emerging freedoms of the countries following the break-up of the Soviet empire has there been established 'heaven on earth' any more than is the case anywhere else in the world. But, while Fukuyama was wrong to think that with the collapse of communism democracy had arrived and the world was safe for human flourishing for ever, it is true that more people are beginning to have the opportunity to be themselves as persons, to take part in public life and to act on the assumption that the future does not have to be like the past.[6] The world is, as we believe, in our hands, provided our intentions are directed towards the fulfilment of God's purpose and we understand that God has all the time in the world to win our support.

The implication is that learning to hope is a lifelong vocation. So when Fukuyama revised his thinking to draw attention to the centrality of trust in all relationships – national, international, social and personal – he was on to something of central importance.[7] It is also a dimension of public life that the Church, in the light of its faith, can wholeheartedly encourage. All things cohere in Christ, the Word through whom all things were made. Far from it being the case that human success depends upon the Church or any other body putting together things that are apart, human success is built upon the ready recognition that all things hang together and work so as to enable human flourishing. It is increasingly obvious with regard to the physical world, as we have seen; the world is one organic set of interacting sets of relations; the movement of a butterfly wing in Brazil affects the movement of the tennis ball on the centre court in a Wimbledon final. We seem to be able to understand that we have heard what the world is saying to us, though we may not acknowledge it as we could and should in the way we live our lives. But when it comes to human society we are far from recognizing let alone acknowledging the implications. We seem deaf to the conversation of the generations that bears witness to the global coherence of human society, let alone being able to understand its significance for human flourishing and seek to embody it in conversations that will lead to mutually advantageous decisions. The success of each nation depends upon the success of every other; yet we still assume that national success will be the product of gaining a competitive advantage whereby a state will secure its own interests at the expense of others.

There was a time in the eighteenth century when it was assumed that since gold was in limited supply, and gold was the standard by which all other wealth was judged, the state that possessed most gold and controlled the trade would be the most powerful. This was succeeded by the view that since international trade was of a relatively fixed quantity, the state that wanted to gain supremacy would have to control the trade routes. We know that neither of these views is true: gold may be limited in quantity, but its use is largely for decorative purposes and so hardly matters except to the jeweller and the speculator; but trade is infinitely expansible. Success for each country means empowering all to take part. As in conversation so in trade – the broader and fuller it is, the more mutually beneficial. In turn this means strengthening local economies, facilitating the building of infrastructures, legal frameworks, ending corruption and, as Fukuyama averred, establishing trust.

It was Hegel who remarked, 'What experience and History teach us is this – that people and governments never have learned anything from history, or acted on principles derived from it.'[8] There seems a depressing amount of truth in his assertion. And indeed much disappointing experience will test the assumption that one will be wise to trust others. Of course, *we* know we can be trusted; what worries us is whether we can trust anyone else. Trust holds things together but it has to be encouraged. When a couple abandons their affectionate language in addressing one another this jeopardizes the mutual trustworthiness they have for each other; it is the same between states and organizations. Trust has to be worked at and embodied in word and action if it is to be recognized. It exists and grows when we look out for one another, engage one another in conversation, and build each other up.

The Church knows that this is what God does in his redemptive creativity; he affirms his commitment, his trustworthiness and his trust in the world, in word and action. We share this in eucharistic celebration, and therefore, in principle, have the strength to bear witness to the trust that lies behind all human life properly lived. We know that this is the case; we do not have to invent it for ourselves. The world relies on the community of faith to demonstrate in its own life the truth of the claim that things do cohere and that all people, personally, are bound together. We believe that the Church includes everyone, that each person depends upon all others and that life is more satisfactory and fulfilling for everyone when that is understood and acknowledged in practice. To hear the gospel is to understand that this is the case, and to set about the business of working it out together in the long-term interests of human flourishing. The Church untiringly affirms that the basis of future hope lies in this God-given reality. If, on the other hand, we think that the only way to succeed is to keep what we have and only to invest when it is for our benefit, we shall be denying the truth of our mutuality and supporting the false view that our success depends upon the failure of others. It is, as Balusariya has said, as inconsistent to believe that one can keep what one has and trade at the expense of others as it is to believe that one can share the grace of God's presence in Christ at the Eucharist and not live it out in one's life.

We can't measure it either. The application of scientific method and mathematical analysis, so beneficial in principle in the investigation of our physical environment, has been catastrophic when applied neat to the matter of social policy and human flourishing. Personal behaviour, economic activity and community life cannot be reduced to numbers. Economic analysis and mathematical calculation will give one valuable information about what is going on, and provide tools that we can use to test policies that we might try in the future, in order to bring benefit to everyone. In personal life it is clear that wealth does not equate with happiness; no more does it with a business or with a national economy. Many successful businesses are unhappy places to work; many wealthy countries are distressed societies; many persons with all the trappings of a prosperous life are inadequate and without friends. Without the lively presence of trust in a family, in a business, in a state and between states, between races, between religions, we shall be unable to establish relationships that reflect the fact of our experience of the world's oneness, or the purpose of God in his creating. What God expressed in his gracious decision to create was not only his faith that the world was good, but also his trust in human persons to rise to the challenge of getting to know him, one another, and the world of which they were a part, so as to be partners in his creation. When we do that, we know what true happiness is.

And so we come to a difficult question. Is the Church in good shape to offer an example to the world at large? Does it behave in such a way as to manifest in itself the authority that it attributes to God? Does it instantiate in its thinking, speaking and acting, the essential value that the Christian tradition attributes to graced human nature? Mostly it does act with appropriate concern and authority: but too often it has not and does not. It would be difficult to affirm its perfection, even if one wanted to. There have been recent occasions for public disquiet: child abuse in the Roman Catholic Church; a threat of schism over homosexuality in the Anglican Communion; a suspicion of corruption in property management in the Orthodox Church; and letters in the *Methodist Recorder* have produced evidence of the bullying of ministers by some in positions of trust in the Church.

Too frequently, the lust for power and a desire to be seen to be exercising it overcomes responsible decision-making; literal compliance with canon law outweighs pastoral concern; and defence of the institution of the Church replaces the central task of bearing witness to God's loving presence in the world. God's authority is authoritative not authoritarian; Christ bears in his body the cost of this relationship. If the Church is to live in conformity with God's world, it will follow the same sacrificial example and act with the same respect. Canon law, as Robert Ombres OP, a distinguished canon lawyer, avers, is pastoral theology in action, not a means whereby petty minds contrive to get their own way.

When Charles Davis abandoned the Roman Catholic Church he did so on grounds of conscience; he could no longer find it in him to recommend participation in the life of a community that he had come to believe stifled human flourishing. It lived by law, he believed, to the exclusion of the Spirit. He was, I believe, wrong theologically; the Church is born of the love of God and that is its staple diet, but it is undeniable that many people experience the exercise of power within the Church in this way. If a legal system is rolled out without concern for the person, one misunderstands the nature of law.

But the weakness and sin of the Church is paradoxically encouragement. It is no part of the doctrine of the Church that it is perfect, only that in the end its proleptic celebration of the unity of all things and all people in Christ will be realized. In the meantime, as a human institution the Church shares the same defects, weaknesses, illnesses and pain as the rest of the world. In what other condition could it possibly present the world to God in Christ? The purpose of the Church is to bear witness to God in the world, not to exercise, in God's name, power over the world or to draw attention to itself. Not even the Church will frustrate the human spirit. God will see to that.

There are two further areas of concern in our human environment that crucially impact in the public mind on the ability of the Church to fulfil its purpose, its disunity and its relationships with other religions. The desire for unity, a common feeling among Christians for many decades, will only be attended to properly if we understand that we are trying to show how things are one, not trying to put together pieces of a jigsaw that do not fit together. Negotiation is a very weak form of conversation since each participant is likely to be focusing on protecting their own interests rather than trying to share with others the vision that holds us together and is at the heart of the desire to be one. But the Church is one: if what the Christian faith has to say about God in his redemptive creativity is true, then the world is already one in Christ. We proclaim this fact eternally in eucharistic celebration. What we do not understand is how to say it in action, how to be one, what it means for our life together and how we can share its power with the whole of creation.

In like manner, we can assert our one community of faith with all persons of faith, and none. The fact is that there are other religious traditions than the Christian, and they are alive and flourishing; no amount of kidding ourselves will lead us to believe really that our job as Christians is to get them all to church. At least I can't believe it. On the contrary, the conversation that God has begun with his world is a conversation that already includes all people in principle, all Christians, all persons of all faiths and of none; our task is therefore to get to know other traditions so that we can begin to find a language in which we can work together in the long-term interests of the common good. For it must be plain to us all that if we do not live and work together as faithful people we shall die separately in the shroud of our own private beliefs.

This is not woolly liberalism, though it is liberal; the doctrines of each religion are not equally true or equally capable of promoting 'the good life'. But profound disagreement about the truth does not mean that there can be no friendship. It is, after all, not the mark of true friendship if you have never quarrelled; good friends should be capable of having a good argument without resort to ridicule, the assertion of power or the attempt to dominate. As a matter of fact, I wish to defend in public conversation with all traditions that the truth of God is centred on Christ and that salvation is through him. But I wish to do so with full awareness of the fact that since all things were created through the Word, there is already an implicit oneness in Christ that we must grasp and find ways of expressing. Jacques Dupuis SJ got himself temporarily into trouble with the Congregation of the Doctrine of the Faith for suggesting that the Church needed to think through again the doctrine of the incarnation.[9] What does it mean to say that all things exist through Christ and at the same time to recognize that there are other traditions alive *within* his present Lordship that we have to come to terms with if we are to gain full insight into the breadth and depth of God's commitment in Christ to making a success of his creation?

If we are serious about including everyone in our conversation with God, there must be no limits; if we want to include everyone, of course we can because the Word of God to us is that in principle they are already included. What better basis could there be on which we can indeed expect to learn to hope?

9

You Can't Keep a Good God Down, Can You?

I have suggested that God, in creating, began a conversation with his world and invited humankind to accept responsibility for pursuing it on behalf of the world. Humankind, I also suggested, finds itself quite naturally inclined to search for meaning in life; it is, I believe, this search that signifies the taking up of God's invitation to join in conversation with him. The conversation involves engagement with the world's processes, puzzlement about our own place in the scheme of things and a desire to listen to one another. It issues in a concern to do something worthwhile to improve the world's lot.

Our conversation with the world, with ourselves, with one another and with God has three products. The first is wisdom, the embodiment of worthwhile experience in good habits of thought and the virtues of good behaviour. The second is the nourishment of love, for only if we love that which we desire to understand will we have the will to pursue the truth that we say we want. The third is hope because all profitable conversation ends with the expectation that the good signs we have identified can be made more of for the benefit of all. Above all, good conversation requires attention to the other and the overcoming of the fear that lies behind the debilitating temptation to assert ourselves. This is profoundly so in respect of conversation with God, conversation with the world and conversation with another person, for only in careful listening will we hear the beauty of holiness, the still, small voice of God. Wisdom and love, the products of shared interest, are lived out in hope and tested in public life.

The Christian tradition gives voice to this worldly insight. Christian theology, aware of the inner yearning of the human soul for meaning and purpose in life, explores the nature of God the Redemptive Creator, affectionately committed to conversation with his world so as to hear its voice and meet its needs. God's wisdom is embodied in the love he expresses for the world in Christ, in the hope for the world that is grounded in Christ and in the encouragement he gives by the power of the Holy Spirit. God wills to allow his truth to take root in the world freely and therefore does not impose himself on the world; indeed he could not and be true to himself, or therefore, his purpose in creating.

The form that God's commitment of himself to the world in Christ takes is the Church, the Body of Christ. In its nature it embodies the wisdom, love and hope of God for his world, in conversation with God, the world and other people. As such it embraces already in principle all that is good and beautiful and true, just and of good report. It is called to express this truth in its life and therefore to bear the pain of making a reality of what it embodies 'really', because only by so doing will it continue in its own body the work of Christ. To be the Church will bring temptation, especially the temptation to despair and to follow the ways of the world instead of following in Christ's footsteps. The Church is therefore *semper reformanda*, always in process of necessary reform.

The Christian believer can never draw the final conclusion to the proof that he is putting together in the search for meaning, and say *quod erat demonstrandum*, for to do so would be to limit the depth of God's giving of himself. Rather, the Christian has the pleasure to say, as affirmed above, *dubito ergo sum*. It is because we are free to doubt that there still lives in us the desire to grow in knowledge and love of God, of his world, of ourselves and of one another. The community of faith is a seeking community, a pilgrim people, the adopted children of God, the Body of Christ, in which all who are looking for God will find him.

What it means for the Church to present all people and the one world to God, and to represent God's presence in the world in Christ, is developed in its searching and in its one conversation with God in Christ. It requires fully self-conscious, committed reflection, and very hard work. But if engaged in openly, optimistically and affectionately, it will result in building up the deposit of wisdom, love and hope on which the world depends for its well-being.

Such a vocation, God-given as it is, naturally arouses fear. What if we fail? And look, there are plenty of signs that the Church is failing! So perhaps it should take action. Should it have an evangelistic campaign? Should it appeal for state support because of all the good works it does? Should we demand that the world should do what we say? Two parables in their contrasting ways bear materially on these questions: the parable of the talents and the parable of the unjust steward.

The parable of the talents concerns a master who is going away and so is unable to retain hands-on control of his investments.[1] He divides the work between three managers and gives one five talents, another two, and a third one. He has complete trust in them but sensibly only gives them responsibilities commensurate with their abilities. On his return the first reports very satisfactory accounts: five talents wisely invested and the capital doubled. The same is true for the second manager: two invested wisely and four now safely banked. They are immediately rewarded and invited to enter into the joy of their master. The third fellow knew well how hard and difficult his master was and so in fear hid the talent entrusted to him. When the master returned he thankfully gave it back to him and breathed a sigh of relief. Responsibility over? Not really! He ducked all the issues.

On reflection, we can see why. This self-regarding manager knew neither the master nor the value of the talent, nor did he recognize the trust that the master had put in him and his performance. His master was not hard or indifferent, but totally committed to his servant's success. He had not been over-burdened with duties he could not fulfil, for the master had given him everything he needed to be successful. He had underestimated his own worth and ability and tried to avoid the responsibility that properly was his. In so doing he had excluded himself from the joy of his master. There are clues here that could assist the Church's self-understanding. Indeed, can we not see the Church here? Certainly in looking at success and failure the Church must recognize the real nature of its Lord and Master, and the fact that the Church is in possession of everything it needs to fulfil its purpose; self-regarding underestimation of its true nature as the Body of Christ will get it nowhere. Entering into the joy of the Lord, making real the relationship it already has with him through his commitment to it, that is something open to the Church here and now and all the time.

The parable of the unjust steward is interesting too. A man is in debt for a stupendous sum and is summoned to pay up. He can't and the king orders him to be bankrupted, which at the time meant the sale of everything he had, including his wife and family into slavery. He begs for time to pay, and the king, seeing his circumstances, out of pity graciously forgives him the lot! Let off the hook – he is thrilled at the power of his own words: he's a winner! On his way home the fellow comes across a colleague who owes him a trifling sum. 'Pay up,' he says. The man pleads for time, but the unjust steward refuses and pursues him with the full force of the law, and the man is imprisoned. Others are unhappy about this and report the steward to the king, who calls him back. The king berates him for his failure to understand and sends him to prison until he has paid up every last penny. Any more clues here? I think so.

The Church of which much is required is also the Church that has been forgiven much. Moreover, its forgiveness did not come about as a result of its well-chosen golden words or shrewd exercise of power, but out of the very nature of God himself. To assume on the basis of its own forgiven state that it can lord it over the world is simply to misunderstand the nature of God to whom it is indebted for its life. The world that Christians know is constituted of colleagues, not servants.

But sad to say, in the face of apparent failure, the Church is inclined to look for self-preservation and self-justification. We have to remind ourselves that the Church is not called in its life to bear witness to itself, live on its own resources or have flashy external marks that indicate to the world that all is well. The Church will not depend upon sound investment policies, more cash in the collections, fine buildings, an increased number of clergy, better discipline and careful obedience to authority, larger congregations, evident power and influence in society, the subtlety of its political manoeuvring, or indeed its good works. They all have their place; they may even be said to be necessary conditions for a well-managed life, though I doubt whether all of them are. What matters is the Church's religious life, the attention to God that this requires of it, and the regular reminder in worship of the nature and presence of God who has committed himself to making a success of his world. The Church is not itself when calling the attention of the world to itself, but when as the community of faith it celebrates God's presence, engages in conversation with him and invites everyone else to join with them. That is enough, if it is done properly.

But this is just what is so difficult. Religion is often misunderstood, and so pushed to one side. Some historians seem to be capable of ignoring the religious dimension of religion in historical enquiry. Thus a distinguished ecclesiastical historian believed Donatism to be a local nationalist movement.[2] In fact it arose from serious concern for the purity of the Church; the Donatists refused to accept Caecilian, Bishop of Carthage, on the grounds that he was consecrated by a *traditor*, Felix of Aptunga, who had handed over the Scriptures during the persecutions of Diocletian. The Pilgrimage of Grace (1536–37) is regarded as essentially a social and economic development by many historians, though the most recent account of the period, Bernard's *The King's Reformation*, takes a strongly contrary view and underlines the religious motivation. Those most involved were concerned that true religion was being undermined by the king: they therefore wanted to reject the royal supremacy, reverse the dissolution of the monasteries and confirm their right and duty to practise their religion in the traditional way.[3] More generally, Maurice Cowling suggests that the move from religious – indeed a Christian – culture to a more secular one, has led historians to lose the language of faith and thus the ability to pick up the continuing influence of Christianity upon the public doctrine of modern England.[4] There is no reason for the Church itself to follow the same false line. The task of the Church is to make a reality of God's presence with his world by engaging society in the widest possible sense, in conversation with God.

The Church is not only counter-cultural in wanting to point to the reality of God, and to involve him in the life of the world; it is counter-cultural in putting the values of conversation at the heart of its programme. Children are fortunate if they have the stimulus of immersion in lively adult conversation. Families eat and talk less together, and watch television in silence; the school environment is dominated by the language of peers around familiar themes such as football or of teachers who have little time for ordinary conversation with students, focused as they are perforce on performance indicators and school league tables. As Stephen Miller has it in the title of his recent book on conversation, it is a declining art.[5] Certainly, as he reports, we must remember, to be fair, that David Hume and Dr Johnson agree that there is no greater enemy of conversation than the religious enthusiast! The way in which one can be bludgeoned by the power of self-righteous rhetoric so that no crack is left through which to squeeze a sensible word has to be experienced to be believed. But then, as R. M. Hare shows in his discussion of toleration and fanaticism, it is the purpose of the fanatic to deny the possibility of falsehood and therefore to ignore every other point of view.[6] The fanatic is determined to exclude the very possibility of conversation.

However, the Church is freed from the need to be enthusiastic in this sense, and certainly from any call to fanaticism, by the enjoyment of the sheer love that God has for the world and its flourishing, and which by God's grace it shares. Its faith is based upon a view of God as committed to the whole world, and only to the institution of the Church as an embodiment of his commitment to the whole world. The Church is free to take an interest in whatever is going on, and whatever the worlds of human enquiry and analysis are yielding, with the purpose of revealing the implicit wisdom, love and hope that will arise through linking them with its conversation with God.

This is an intellectual task, though as we shall see not simply an intellectual one. The resources are huge: the Church neglects most of them. I fear this is because it is self-regarding and focused upon the public reputation engendered by its desire to be seen to be successful or the determination to insist on legal rights. Look at us! But neither transient approbation such as Jesus had in entering Jerusalem, or the niceties of a legal claim such as that of the unjust steward, will give substance to the Church's witness to God. The value of this claim, indeed its sole value, lies in its truth. What does the Church's faith amount to? Is it true? It is even essential to take seriously the hoary question about the existence of God, so often dismissed as unintelligible or impossible to answer. Does God exist? How would you set about dealing with these questions? They are frequently ignored as irrelevant or dealt with in naive responses that cut no ice with anyone. They require serious intellectual attention.

We show so little interest in them, partly, I think, because the intellectual life is undervalued and regarded with suspicion. 'Such men are dangerous – and a nuisance!' The English tend to think, rather proudly, that this is a characteristic of English society because we flatter ourselves that we are thoroughly pragmatic and realistic and don't waste our time on trifles or questions that have no answer. Harold Wilson, the former British prime minister, had the habit of dismissing an argument that he did not want to attend to as 'theological', by which of course he meant that the answer would make no difference to the outcome as he saw it. But as far as the Church is concerned it is precisely the theological questions that matter most. For if indeed we can make sense of the Christian tradition, *and it is true*, then by uncovering its implicit links with human experience of the world in all its dimensions it will nourish our awareness of one another as capable of working together for the common good.

Actually, the dismissive attitude to the intellectual life mistakes its nature and purpose. Descartes said that books had nourished him ever since he was a child.[7] Quite right too! But not only books, as Descartes pointed out and as I have had occasion to emphasize already. The confusion is natural but mistaken; the product of the intellectual life is not book learning, but habits of thought that enable a critical awareness of truth and falsity, what is worth attending to and what is not, how to behave and how not to behave. These fruits will not be recorded in certificates or diplomas, they will be written in lives. We want the word of the expert, but we will be sensible to consider the advice and then decide for ourselves what we are going to do in the light of it. And in any case we all know the Latin tag, *quot homines, tot sententiae* – 'there are as many opinions as there are people' – especially when applied to the case of economists! So we have little choice but to accept the responsibility of being human and make up our minds. All of us in one way or another are living the intellectual life, and trying to work things out. Indeed, as we might better say, we are all trying to live out the truth as we see it in full knowledge of the fact that we need one another if we are even vaguely to approach it.

Hence the essential nature of genuine conversation involves the whole self, as will any form of learning. *Conversazione* is a 'walking round together with', as Socrates did with friends in the academy, engaging with one another, talking, observing, debating, arguing, including, rejecting, believing, hoping. Conversation involves taking other people seriously, debating what they have to say for themselves, widening the circle, living what one is beginning to understand for oneself and judging it again in the light of experience. Human conversation began at the dawn of history and has continued ever since. The conversation of the Church continues this human conversation with God; it does not depend for its continuity on its own strength but on the reality of the God whose world this is, whose Son called the Church into existence, and whose Spirit encourages its life. Tissa Balasuriya urges the Church to bear witness to the Holy Spirit in the world and not to attempt the (fortunately) impossible task of confining the Spirit within the Church and trying to earn its right to exist by rationing it to others.[8]

God bears witness to his essential nature and of the value he attributes to the world in his commitment of himself to the world. The Church will likewise find its essential nature in following God's example and committing itself to the world in conversation so that it and the whole world may enter into the glorious liberty of the children of God.

Ella Fitzgerald was right to sing in the fine words and music of George and Ira Gershwin: 'Love is Here to Stay', and 'They Can't Take That Away From Me'. God affirms the first in Christ, and we affirm the second in faith. In so doing we are learning to hope. As Julian of Norwich wrote, 'All shall be well and all manner of thing shall be well.'

You can't keep a good God down, can you? You can try, but no; he is risen! he is risen, indeed! If only we believed it, life would be so much more fun.

Notes

Preface

1 Harry Ayres, title of an article in which he paid tribute to one of his teachers recently deceased. *Financial Times*, 18/19 February, 2006.

2 *The Catholic Catechism*, London, Burns and Oates, 1994.

3 *Common Worship*, London, Church House Publishing, 2000.

Introduction

1 Language is often illuminating: one can find financial resources referred to as financial 'strength' and even sometimes financial 'clout'. These terms indicate a reductionist and inappropriate understanding of the real value of wealth, and even more so of the real value of 'social' and 'personal' capital.

2 Nicholas Boyle, *Who Are We Now? Christian Humanism and the Global Market from Hegel to Heaney*, Edinburgh, T & T Clark, 1998.

3 Alan Watson produced for Thames Television a series on Germany post-unification, *The Germans: Who Are They Now?* A book with the same title appeared (London, Methuen, 1992).

4 I take seriously the invitation which Isaiah puts into the mouth of God, 'Come let us reason together' (Isa. 1.18). It seems a common sense invitation if it is God's intention, as I believe it to be, that we should understand his word, make sense of it and live it out in community in God's world. After all, so far as one can see, Jesus did not set out to determine what his followers should believe; he invited his disciples, and therefore us, to share in conversation – a conversation that will include in perpetuity the Living Word of God, where burgeoning freedom will inspire self-knowledge, an increasing ability to pay attention to the world as it is, a capacity for 'courteous translation', and sympathetic understanding of all other persons alongside whom we stand as members of the human race. Cf. e.g. John 16.12–15, 25–28.

5 Richard Koch and Chris Smith (eds), *The Suicide of the West*, London, Institute of Economic Affairs, 2006. Interestingly the six values to which the book draws attention are Christianity, optimism, science, economic growth, liberalism and individualism.

6 Michael Polanyi, *The Tacit Dimension*, London, Routledge and Kegan Paul, 1966.

7 Michael Polanyi, *Personal Knowledge: Towards a Post-Critical Philosophy*, London, Routledge and Kegan Paul, 1958.

Chapter 1

1 Samuel Beckett, *Waiting for Godot*, London, Faber and Faber, 1956.

2 Shakespeare, *Macbeth* V, v, l.26–28.

3 T. S. Eliot, 'East Coker', *Four Quartets*, London, Faber and Faber, 1944.

4 Michael Oakeshott, 'Education: The Engagement and its Frustration', in Timothy Fuller (ed.), *The Voice of Liberal Learning: Michael Oakeshott on Education*, New Haven and London, Yale University Press, 1989. Michael Oakeshott was a philosopher who after teaching at Cambridge became Professor of Political Science at the London School of Economics (1951–69); he is rightly regarded as the foremost conservative writer on political philosophy of the second half of the twentieth century, perhaps the chief inheritor of the mantle of Edmund Burke (1729–97). His writings on education are especially stimulating and clearly arise from reflection on the actual experience of teaching, and a passionate concern for 'the liberal arts', in which, of course, he included the human exploration of the natural world in the sciences. See also, for example, 'Learning and Teaching' (first published in R. S. Peters, *The Concept of Education*, London, Routledge and Kegan Paul, 1967), and 'A Place of Learning' (1972), also helpfully reprinted in Fuller, *The Voice of Liberal Learning*.

5 There are innumerable reproductions of these paintings in many books. One of the best is in Ronald de Leeuw, *Van Gogh Museum*, Zwolle, Waanders Publishers, no date.

6 Most scholars are now agreed that *creatio ex nihilo* is not a biblical doctrine, though Genesis 1—2 can be read that way; clear expression of such a belief does not occur before the late evidence of 2 Maccabees. The framework of belief about creation in the Old Testament is rather of God's Spirit as the creating presence that brings order to existing recalcitrant, destructive and chaotic forces. In what sense 'existing', it is interesting to speculate! Cf. Walter Brueggemann, *Theology in the Old Testament*, Minneapolis,

Fortress Press, 1997, p. 158 ff., and Chapter 17 passim.

  7 Gen. 1.31a.

Chapter 2

  1 Can 204 #1. *The Canon Law: Letter and Spirit*, London, Geoffrey Chapman, 1995.

  2 It is interesting to reflect upon the extent to which Judaism is essential to Christian understanding. On some accounts the experience of the Jews was a God-determined necessary precursor of Christianity, and Christian Faith its fulfilment. Does this mean that one should talk of one entity – Judaeo-Christianity? I don't think so. Only if one sees Judaism as complete in itself has one the possibility of engaging with it with proper respect; and it is necessary to respect the tradition in order to become aware of one's own position as a Christian. And in any case, if one seeks to understand Christian faith in India or China, does one have first to teach Judaism? Surely not!

  3 See below, especially, Chapters 7 and 8.

  4 1 Kings 17.8–16; 1 Sam. 3.1–18; Jer. 32.

  5 Exod. 34.11–28; Deut. 5.6–21.

  6 Lev. 19.2–4, 17–18.

  7 Pierre Hadot, *Philosophy as a Way of Life*, Oxford, Blackwell, 1995.

  8 Plato, *The Republic*; Aristotle, *Nichomachian Ethics*, *Politics*.

  9 Isa. 1.18.

  10 John Haldane, *Faithful Reason: Essays Catholic and Philosophical*, London, Routledge, 2004, a collection of essays, reflects this theme from a Christian perspective.

  11 See especially G. Ernest Wright, *God Who Acts: Biblical Theology as Recital*, London, SCM Press, 1952.

  12 See the discussion of Thomas Tracy, *God, Action and Embodiment*, Grand Rapids, Eerdmans, 1984.

  13 Exod. 3.6.

  14 Exod. 3.14.

  15 1 Sam. 10.1; 2 Sam. 7.12–13.

  16 Ezek. 34.23.

  17 Ps. 23.1, 6.

  18 Christopher R. North, *The Suffering Servant in Deutero-Isaiah: An Historical and Critical Study*, Oxford, Oxford University Press, 1948, 2nd edn, 1956. Chapter VII, The Songs: Text and Translation, pp. 117–38.

  19 Dan. 7.13–14.

Chapter 3

1 I'm not going to debate their historicity, though I cannot resist commenting that the question of their historicity is as mysterious as their significance. Personally, I do not know whether they occurred or not, because I do not know how to set about the task of proving that they were actual events in the normal history of the world, as we know it. Do you?

2 A contentious opinion, I admit; see below, Chapter 7.

3 I. T. Ramsey, *Religious Language*, London, SCM Press, 1957.

4 Matt. 12.22ff.

5 C. S. Lewis, *The Screwtape Letters*, London, Geoffrey Bles, 1942; Fontana paperback, 1955.

6 Rupert Davies, a former President of the Methodist Conference, once splendidly described it as the first successful anti-litter campaign in history! 'Gather up the fragments left over, so that nothing may be lost' (John 6.12b).

7 John 6.15.

8 John 6.41b.

Chapter 4

1 Mark 8.27. Clearly it was recognized to be an important question by all the Gospel writers. Cf. Matthew 16.13: 'Who do people say that the Son of Man is?' and Luke 9.18: 'Who do the crowds say that I am?' John 6.66–69 seems to be the disciples' response to an analogous question posed by Jesus' behaviour. 'Who am I then?'

2 We shouldn't get over-excited about this; the same could be said of Muslims, supporters of Manchester United and Arsenal, and even, terrible as it seems, flat-earthers!

3 And notwithstanding the fact that most scholars would place the date of Jesus' birth as 3 or 4 BC.

4 Luke 4.9–12.

5 Luke 4.13.

6 Luke 23.46.

7 John 19.30.

8 1 Cor. 15.19.

9 Athanasius, *Festal Epistle* of 387.

10 John 1.5.

11 Rom. 8.31.

12 Rom. 8.38–39.

13 Mark 12.17.

14 Rom. 13.1–7.

15 Matt. 5.31–32.

16 Mark 10.4–9.
17 2 Cor. 6.14–16a.

Chapter 5

1 The words are by Daryl Runswick and Kerry Crabbe. Variously issued, but available on RCA Victor 09026 61664 2.
2 Josh. 6.
3 Lam. 5.21–22.
4 Isa. 42.1–7; 49.1–7; 50.4–9; 52.13—53.12.
5 Mark 10.35–41.
6 Mark 3.1–6.
7 Mark 2.23–28.
8 Mark 2.27–28.
9 Luke 23.42–43.
10 Dietrich Bonhoeffer, *The Cost of Discipleship*, London, SCM Press, 1959.
11 'Theology and Falsification', a discussion between Anthony Flew, R. M. Hare and Basil Mitchell with a concluding essay by I. M. Crombie, in A. G. N. Flew and A. MacIntyre (eds), *New Essays in Philosophical Theology*, London, SCM Press, 1955, pp. 96–130.
12 A. G. N. Flew, 'Divine Omnipotence and Human Freewill', in A. G. N. Flew and A. MacIntyre (eds), *New Essays in Philosophical Theology*, London, SCM Press, 1955, pp. 144–69. Flew himself, while not an orthodox believer in any sense, has said more recently that there is sufficient sense of order in the universe to warrant belief in some Originator of it all.
13 Matt. 28.18–20.
14 Mark 14.22–24.
15 1 Cor. 11.23–25.
16 1 Cor. 13.12–13.
17 1 Cor. 13.13.
18 *Hymns and Songs*, 596, London, Methodist Publishing House, 1983. *Hymns Ancient and Modern: New Standard*, 258, London, Hymns Ancient and Modern Limited, 1983.

Chapter 6

1 John 6.15.
2 Mark 15.34b.
3 Mark 14.36.
4 David Head, *He Sent Leanness*, London, Epworth, 1957.
5 J. Neville Ward, *The Use of Praying*, London, Epworth, 1967.

This must surely be one of the most useful books ever written on the subject.

6 Geoffrey Elton, *Times Literary Supplement*, 2 December 1965.

7 Francis de Sales, *Introduction to the Devout Life*, London, Dent, Everyman's Library 324, p. 51.

8 Phil. 4.4–7.

9 Hans Urs von Balthasar, *The Christian State of Life*, San Francisco, Ignatius Press, p. 68.

10 Jean Pierre de Caussade, SJ, *Abandonment to Divine Providence*, Exeter, Catholic Records Press, 1921.

11 Matt. 5.48.

12 Augustine Baker, OSB, *Holy Wisdom, The Third Treatise: Of Prayer*, Wheathampstead, Anthony Clark Books, 1972, p. 299.

13 Francis de Sales, *Abandonment to Divine Providence*, Exeter, Catholic Records Press, 1921, p. 53.

14 There have been several editions, the most accessible of which is published by Penguin.

15 J. Neville Ward, *Five for Sorrow, Ten for Joy*, London, Epworth, 1971.

16 Cf. John Drury, *Painting the Word*, New Haven and London, Yale University Press, 1999, pp. 32–7.

17 Aquinas, *Summa Contra Gentiles*, 2, ii.

Chapter 7

1 Cf., e.g. John Passmore, *Man's Responsibility for Nature*, London, Duckworth, 1974, Chapter 1, Man as Despot, especially p. 13.

2 Passmore, *Man's Responsibility for Nature*, p. 184.

3 Richard Dawkins, *Unweaving the Rainbow*, London, Penguin, 1998.

4 John Wren-Lewis used to discuss this in the 1960s and 1970s.

5 Aquinas, *Summa Contra Gentiles*, 2, ii.

6 William Paley, *A View of the Evidences of Christianity*, 1794; *Natural Theology*, 1802.

7 For the very best contemporary defence of this position see Robert Merrihew Adams, *Finite and Infinite Goods: A Framework for Ethics*, New York, Oxford University Press, 1999.

8 Quoted in Thomas Torrance, *Einstein and God*, http://www.ctinquiry.org/publications/reflections_volume_1/torrance.htm

9 John Henry Newman, *Essay on the Development of Christian Doctrine*, 1845.

10 John Robinson, *Honest to God*, London, SCM Press, 1963.

Chapter 8

1 Tissa Balasuriya, *Eucharist and Human Liberation*, New York, Orbis, 1979.
2 John 8.7b.
3 John 8.15.
4 John Allegro, a brilliant student of the Semitic languages, came to believe that western religions were a development from the cultic worship of a sacred mushroom. John Allegro, *The Sacred Mushroom and the Cross*, Garden City, New York, Doubleday, 1970.
5 Ernst van Alphen, *Francis Bacon and the Loss of Self*, London, Reaktion Books, 1992.
6 Francis Fukuyama, *The End of History and The Last Man*, London, Penguin, 1992.
7 Francis Fukuyama, *Trust*, London, Penguin, 1996.
8 G. W. F. Hegel, *Philosophy of History*, trans. J. Sibree, New York, 1956, Introduction.
9 Jacques Dupuis, SJ, *Toward a Christian Theology of Religious Pluralism*, Maryknoll, New York, Orbis, 1997, and *Christianity and the Religions From Confrontation to Dialogue*, London, Darton Longman and Todd, 2002.

Chapter 9

1 Matt. 25.14–30.
2 W. H. C. Frend, *The Donatist Church: A Movement of Protest in Roman North Africa*, Oxford, 1952, 3rd edn, 1985.
3 M. L. Bush, *The Pilgrimage of Grace*, Manchester, Manchester University Press, 1996. R. W. Hoyle, *The Pilgrimage of Grace*, Oxford, Oxford University Press, 2001. In contrast, see G. W. Bernard, *The King's Reformation: Henry VIII and the Remaking of the English Church*, New Haven and London, Yale University Press, 2005.
4 Maurice Cowling, *Religion and Public Doctrine in Modern England*, Volume 1, Cambridge, Cambridge University Press, 1980.
5 Stephen Miller, *Conversation: A History of a Declining Art*, New Haven and London, Yale University Press, 2006.
6 R. M. Hare, *Freedom and Reason*, Oxford, Oxford University Press, 1963, pp. 159–85.
7 Rene Descartes, *Discourse on Method*, Bk vi, 4.
8 Tissa Balasuriya, 'Liberation of the Holy Spirit', *Ecumenical Review*, 43 (1991), pp. 200–05.